NOTTIN FOREST F.C.

- THE 25 YEAR RECORD

1970-71 to 1994-95 Seasons

SEASON BY SEASON WRITE-UPS
David Powter

EDITOR
Michael Robinson

CONTENTS

British Library Cataloguing in Publication Data
A catalogue record for this book is available from the British Library
ISBN 0-947808-61-2

Copyright © 1995; SOCCER BOOK PUBLISHING LTD. (01472-696226)
72, St. Peters' Avenue, Cleethorpes, Sth. Humberside, DN35 8HU, England

Printed by Redwood Books, Kennet House, Kennet Way, Trowbridge, Wilts.

NOTTINGHAM FOREST
- Seasons 1970-71 to 1994-95

When Nottingham Forest finished third in the FA Carling Premiership in 1994-95, their prospects looked so much brighter than at the start of 1970-71, 25 seasons before. They were also a top-flight side then, but in between have experienced two spells in the second-flight. They have also had by far the most glorious period in their history.

Managed by Matt Gillies, Forest started 1970-71 as an average First Division side and that season did nothing to change their mediocre rating. They finished the campaign in 16th, one place lower than the previous term. Gillies' shot-shy side scored at a rate of exactly one per game, and in 10 out of 11 consecutive early season games failed to score at all. Only Ian Moore (with 18) and Peter Cormack (with 7) netted more than 3 times. A remarkable feature in 1970-71 was that goalkeeper Jim Barron and the whole of his defence (Peter Hindley, John Winfield, Bob Chapman and Liam O'Kane) were ever-present.

The defence was neither ever-present nor particularly good in 1971-72 when it leaked 81 goals as Forest slipped into the Second Division for the first time in 15 years. Only 4 matches were won before Christmas and 7 defeats on the reel early in the new year effectively sealed their fate. Tommy Gemmell's arrival (from Celtic) perked them up, but the revival was too little, too late and they finished 4 points short of safety in 21st place. Moore was again the top scorer with 13, despite his March move to Old Trafford.

Forest were one of the early Second Division pace-makers in 1972-73; but a spate of defeats tested the crowd's patience. By the middle of October Gillies' position became untenable. The new manager, Dave Mackay, made few changes and even less impact on the team's form and they finished 14th. An inability to put the ball in the net was again the major problem. There were 4 joint top scorers with 6 goals apiece - Duncan McKenzie, Martin O'Neill, Neil Martin and John Galley.

Despite a mixed start to 1973-74, Forest were among the leaders when Mackay moved to a similar position at Derby. His replacement was Allan Brown, the Bury boss. Mackay's last signing, Ian Bowyer, began to put some pep into the side but the real star was the emerging McKenzie who netted 26 goals. However, Brown's side could not quite penetrate the top three and finished 7th, 4 points short of promotion.

Nevertheless, they grabbed some glory in 1973-74 by reaching the quarter-final of the FA Cup, beating Manchester City along the way. Another First Division side Newcastle, were their opponents in the last eight and that St James' Park clash turned out to be one of the most controversial in the competition's history. Forest were leading 2-1 when they were awarded a second half penalty. A Newcastle player was dismissed for protesting and after George Lyall converted the kick the referee had to take the players off because of a pitch invasion. The game resumed after an 8 minute break and Newcastle scored three times to make it 4-3. However, the match was quickly annulled by the FA and was replayed at Goodison Park 9 days later. There were no goals in that next match, but it was the Magpies who eventually progressed by winning a 'third' tie 1-0, when the teams returned to Goodison Park 3 days later.

Brown's tenure at the City Ground ended the following January, after his side failed to make any impact on the leaders. Brian Clough was immediately installed as the manager. His first transfer dealings were to recruit John McGovern and John O'Hare, both of whom had played for him before, at three and two other clubs, respectively. Forest went on to win only 3 of the last 17 games of 1974-75, but were never in serious relegation danger and finished 16th, 6 points clear of the drop.

A newcomer to the City Ground during the summer of 1975 was full-back Frank Clark, who had been freed by Newcastle. Forest got off to a mixed start in 1975-76 and hardly improved, sitting in mid-division, until a late burst took them up to 8th.

Peter Taylor rejoined his former boss to become assistant manager in July

1976 and his arrival, together with those of striker Peter Withe (from Birmingham) and Coventry's centre-half Larry Lloyd, seemed to have a significant affect on Forest's fortunes. After a mediocre start, it soon became apparent that exciting times were just around the corner as they got into the flow, netting 23 times in 5 successive high scoring victories at the City Ground. Three away games were lost in between, but gradually their form on the road also picked up. A brief blip, when they let Luton and Notts County win at the City Ground, slowed them down; but 5 straight wins pushed them back into promotion contention. However, they won only 3 of their last 7 games and required assistance from other clubs to secure promotion.

Forest had finished the campaign in a promotion place, third - 4 points ahead of Bolton who, however, had 3 rearranged games to fulfil. They won the first, but then lost 1-0 to the Champions Wolves at Burnden Park. The Trotters' final game was academic as by then they needed to win by a rugby score to take third place and the champagne was already flowing on the banks of the Trent.

Withe finished top scorer with 16, Bowyer netted 12 and Tony Woodcock hit 11. The latter appeared in each of the last 30 games after returning from an early season loan spell at Doncaster.

As a sign of the good things to come, Clough's side won a trophy in that promotion winning 1976-77 campaign. They beat Orient over two legs in the final of the Anglo-Scottish Cup.

A Forest stalwart, Bob Chapman, moved across the Trent to Notts County during the summer of 1977 after 359 League games in a red shirt. Clough had already signed Birmingham's Kenny Burns to take his place, and early in the season added Peter Shilton (from Stoke), and one of his old Derby midfielders, Archie Gemmill.

Clough's side was now taking shape and it took the First Division by storm. To everybody's surprise, Forest won 11 of the first 16 games. Their critics still forecast that the bubble would burst; but it never did. After losing for the third time on 19th November, they went 26 games without defeat to finish as Champions with 64 points - 7 more than the runners-up Liverpool. Only four other clubs had accumulated more points in winning the Championship since the Second World War.

It was the second time that Clough (and Taylor) had turned a Second Division side into Football League Champions within a short space of time, having previously achieved it with Derby. Their skill in the transfer market in enticing Shilton, Burns, Gemmill and Dave Needham (who joined from QPR mid-season) was the key to this latest success. To underline matters, the combative Kenny Burns deservedly collected the 1977-78 'Player of the Year' award.

Withe and John Robertson finished as joint top scorers with 12, while Woodcock (who had another fine campaign) again contributed 11. Clark missed most of the season through injury and the regular full-back pairing was Viv Anderson and Colin Barrett. Lloyd, Bowyer, O'Neill and McGovern were the other regulars in a team that worked so hard for one another.

That team (or eight parts of it) had gained an earlier trophy success in the 1977-78 season. After losing an FA Cup quarter-final at WBA, Forest bounced back to win a League Cup replay. The first game with Liverpool had ended in a goalless stalemate; but a Robertson penalty was enough to secure them their first major trophy in 19 seasons. Shilton, Gemmill and Needham were cup-tied and so 17 year-old goalkeeper Chris Woods and O'Hare were called upon to make valuable contributions and collect winners' medals.

Retaining the League Championship was never going to be easy and it was made even more difficult when they only drew 6 of the first 7 games. Nevertheless, Forest were soon on the tails of the leaders and did not lose until the 17th game, at Liverpool. Withe had moved to Newcastle after just one game and his place was taken first by Steve Elliot, and then, with much more success, by Garry Birtles (who ended up as top scorer with 14). Forest gradually moved through the field, losing just 2 more games, but too many draws prevented them from getting alongside the Champions Liverpool. However, second place was a creditable performance and far from Forest's only reward in 1978-79.

A 3-1 aggregate win over Watford put Clough's side into another League Cup final. This time they did not require a replay, as 2 goals by Birtles and another by Woodcock gave them a 3-2 edge over Southampton.

One man who did not play in that League Cup final was Trevor Francis, who had been purchased mid-season from Birmingham for £1 million and was cup-tied. However, he was eligible for their European Cup campaign and by the time he appeared, Forest had already collected the scalps of Liverpool, AEK Athens, Grasshoppers and Cologne to reach the final. The semi-final meetings with Cologne proved to be their biggest test, a 3-3 draw at the City Ground gave Clough's side an uphill battle in Germany; but Bowyer hit the only goal to make it a night of glory.

Forest's second night of glory in Germany came in the final in Munich against the Swedish Champions Malmö. That, too, ended in a single goal victory. The scorer was Francis with a back-post header in first-half injury-time.

So, just 2 years after scraping into the top-flight on the backs of Bolton's misfortune, Nottingham Forest had been crowned Kings of Europe. Their trophy haul numbered four, during a period when they had not been beaten at the City Ground.

Frank Gray, Asa Hartford and, mid-season, Stan Bowles all joined in 1979-80. Hartford's Forest career lasted just 3 games before he moved on once again.

Brighton became the first side in 52 matches to beat Forest at the City Ground, when they won 1-0 in November. That defeat was one of 5 in 6 games which effectively scuppered their title hopes. It was also Woodcock's last before he moved to Cologne. A late revival lifted them to a 1979-80 finish of 5th and, in the meantime, they reached a third League Cup final after squeezing past West Ham and Liverpool. However, a silly misunderstanding between Needham and Shilton enabled Wolves to take the trophy by a single Andy Gray goal.

The League Cup may have been given away sloppily, but that was not the case in the European Cup. However, they were severely tested by Dynamo Berlin in the quarter-final. The East Germans won 1-0 at the City Ground, but a brace by Francis and a Robertson penalty proved more than enough as the away leg was captured 3-1.

Francis and another Robertson spot-kick gave them a two goal lead against Ajax in the semi-final; and although the Dutch halved the deficit on their own soil they could not force extra-time.

Their opponents in the Madrid final were Hamburg, complete with Kevin Keegan in their ranks. Robertson netted the only goal, but the real hero was Shilton who pulled off a string of fine saves to keep his side in front.

John Robertson scores the only goal in the 1979 European Cup Final against Hamburg in Madrid.

Forest lost their grip on the European Cup in the first round in 1980-81, when CSKA Sofia beat them 1-0 twice. Clough's dreams of a first FA Cup success were fuelled by a run to the quarter-final stage, but were then punctured by Ipswich. Forest failed to win anything that season as several of their new signings failed to produce the goods. Raimondo Ponte, Peter Ward and Einar Aas were all internationals, but none matched the class of their predecessors. Another new boy, Ian Wallace, finished the top scorer with 11 goals as Forest finished 7th.

Wallace was also the top scorer in 1981-82 with 7 goals out of a meagre total of 42. Forest had slumped to 12th and the arrival of Justin Fashanu and Jürgen Rober added little to the cause. Brian Clough was left holding the reins alone, after Peter Taylor retired at the end of the season.

1982-83 was a much better campaign with Colin Todd and Kenny Swain signing to help shore up the defence. After a mixed start, they had climbed into the Championship race by Christmas. However, they could not quite maintain the pressure and finished 5th.

Forest's improvement continued in 1983-84. After another mixed start they steadily moved up the table to second place in February. They again failed to sustain their challenge, but 3 successive victories in May secured them third place, 6 points off the top.

Clough's side also fell just short of glory in the UEFA Cup in 1983-84. They side-stepped Vorwaerts, PSV Eindhoven, Celtic (with a fine win at Parkhead) and Sturm Graz to set up semi-final meetings with Anderlecht. Two goals by Steve Hodge gave Forest the edge in the first leg, but the Belgians fought back to win 3-0 on their own soil.

Forest's next UEFA Cup campaign also foundered in Belgium, this time at the first hurdle, with FC Bruges winning 1-0 on aggregate. The club also slipped backwards in the League in 1984-85; a good start enabled them to head the early tables, but they lost form and finished 9th. Peter Davenport was the top scorer with 16.

That honour went to Nigel Clough (with 15 goals) a year later, with his father's side improving one place to 8th. They made a poor start, but 5 straight wins lifted them to mid-table where they stayed for the remainder of 1985-86.

Forest also finished 8th in 1986-87, but this was a very disappointing outcome after they had been serious title challengers for the first 4 months. They won 11 of the first 18 fixtures and stood in second place in early December. However, their challenge crumbled amongst a glut of draws and they won just 7 of their remaining 24 games.

Another title challenge was mounted in 1987-88, on the back of 13 victories in 1987. However, their hopes again faded in the second half of the campaign and they finished a distant third. In the FA Cup, a fine 2-1 victory at Highbury took Clough's side into the last four, but it was Liverpool who progressed to the final, after one of the best semi-finals for years.

That semi-final was held at Hillsborough; one year later the two sides returned their for a rerun. However, the game had to be abandoned following the worst tragedy in British sporting history (with 96 spectators killed and over two hundred injured). Liverpool won the hollow 'replay' 3-1 at Old Trafford.

Six days before the Hillsborough disaster, Forest won the League (now the Littlewoods) Cup with a 3-1 victory over Luton. Nigel Clough netted twice and made a third for Neil Webb. The club also won another cup at Wembley in 1988-89, beating Everton 4-3 after extra-time in the Simod Cup.

After a disappointing start, Forest had made headway in the League in 1988-89, with 6 consecutive victories around the turn of the year. A fruitful spring enabled them to finish third again, 12 points behind the top two.

Another mixed start hampered their challenge the following term, but a 9 game unbeaten run lifted them into third place in early March. However, 6 defeats in seven sent them backwards and it needed 3 victories from the last 4 games to secure 9th place. Forest returned to Wembley in 1989-90 to retain the Littlewoods Cup. A single goal by Nigel Jemson was enough to beat Oldham and secure the club their fourth League Cup.

Just over a year later, red and white scarves again headed to Middlesex for Forest's first FA Cup final in 32 years. A Stuart Pearce free-kick gave them a half-time lead, but their opponents Spurs equalised; and then won in extra-time through an unfortunate Des Walker own-goal.

There were few highlights in Forest's 1990-91 League season but, after being mid-division most of the campaign, they lifted themselves up to finish 8th, through a 16 point haul from the last 6 games.

They also finished 8th a year later, again after being in mid-table most of the season. The club was involved in 3 long cup runs in 1991-92 and visited Wembley twice. However, Brian Clough was destined not to enjoy FA Cup success and a single Portsmouth goal knocked his side out at the quarter-final stage. One goal also ended Forest's hopes in the Rumbelows Cup final, with Manchester United being the victors. Their only trophy success was the Zenith Data Systems Cup, by a 3-2 margin over Southampton in the final.

1992-93 was a disastrous season as - after a span of 16 seasons in the top-flight - Nottingham Forest were relegated. They won the opening game, but then secured only 2 more victories from the next twenty. Five wins in seven briefly revived hopes of survival in early 1993, but only 2 more victories were forthcoming and they finished in 22nd and bottom place, 9 points adrift of safety.

Brain Clough resigned at the end of the season, after 18 years as the club's manager. Until his arrival, Nottingham Forest had only won 2 major trophies (the FA Cup twice) in their history. He led them to 7 more - the Football League title, 2 European Cups and 4 League Cups. He was the 'Manager of the Year' in 1977-78.

The other Clough, Brian's son Nigel, also left the City Ground before the start of 1993-94. He moved to Liverpool after 311 League games in which he netted 101 times. He was the club's top scorer in 6 out of the 8 full

Reknowned as a manager, Brian Clough was also the fastest player to score 200 League goals, taking only 219 League games to do so - almost a goal a game!

seasons in which he was a member of the first team.

The man given the difficult job of filling Brian Clough's shoes was one of his former players, Frank Clark. He had been Leyton Orient's Managing Director for two years after previously managing them for eight.

After a disappointing start, Clark started to enjoy getting his hands dirty again. His new side won only twice in the first 9 matches, but gradually improved before a 13 game unbeaten run pushed them into promotion contention. Having got the bit between their teeth, Forest stormed back into the Premiership. They lost just one of their last 16 matches to finish as runners-up to long-term leaders Crystal Palace. The total of 83 points was the biggest haul in the club's history.

Stan Collymore was the 1993-94 top scorer (with 19) in his first year at the City Ground, while the main fulcrum for the side's success had been the solidity of a defence containing Pearce, Des Lyttle, Colin Cooper and Steve Chettle.

Collymore followed with another 22 goals in 1994-95 as his side took the Premiership by surprise. Collymore had been joined up front by Dutch international Bryan Roy; and the midfield of Lars Bohinen, Steve Stone, David Phillips and Ian Woan was superb. With goalkeeper Mark Crossley and his defence conceding less than a goal per game, Frank Clark's side finished third, only 10 points behind the Champions Blackburn, and gained a UEFA Cup place.

Redevelopment of the ground nearing completion. With an all-seater capacity of over 30,000 the City Ground is among the best in the Country.

1970-71

1	Aug	15	(h)	Coventry C	W 2-0	Lyons, Storey-Moore	25,137
2		18	(h)	West Brom A	D 3-3	Lyons, Rees, Cormack	24,423
3		22	(a)	Ipswich T	D 0-0		19,152
4		26	(a)	Newcastle U	D 1-1	Storey-Moore	34,960
5		29	(h)	Wolverhampton W	W 4-1	Hindley, Newton, Rees, Storey-Moore (pen)	24,343
6	Sep	2	(a)	Stoke C	D 0-0		13,951
7		5	(a)	Crystal Palace	L 0-2		26,510
8		12	(h)	Manchester C	L 0-1		28,896
9		19	(a)	Liverpool	L 0-3		40,675
10		26	(h)	Leeds U	D 0-0		31,537
11	Oct	3	(a)	Arsenal	L 0-4		32,053
12		10	(h)	Blackpool	W 3-1	Lyons, Rees, Cormack	16,618
13		17	(a)	Coventry C	L 0-2		25,392
14		24	(a)	Huddersfield T	D 0-0		17,121
15		31	(h)	Tottenham H	L 0-1		25,301
16	Nov	7	(a)	Everton	L 0-1		39,525
17		14	(h)	Manchester U	L 1-2	Cormack	36,364
18		21	(a)	Burnley	L 1-2	Storey-Moore	13,036
19		28	(h)	Derby Co	L 2-4	Chapman, Storey-Moore	30,539
20	Dec	5	(a)	Southampton	L 1-4	Cormack	19,016
21		12	(h)	Chelsea	D 1-1	Storey-Moore	20,080
22		19	(h)	Ipswich T	L 0-1		14,085
23	Jan	9	(a)	West Brom A	W 1-0	Storey-Moore	20,416
24		16	(h)	Newcastle U	W 2-1	Storey-Moore 2	21,798
25	Feb	6	(h)	Southampton	W 2-0	Storey-Moore, Collier	18,009
26		17	(a)	Chelsea	L 0-2		19,339
27		20	(h)	Burnley	W 1-0	Storey-Moore	20,858
28		24	(a)	West Ham U	L 0-2		35,601
29	Mar	6	(h)	Huddersfield T	L 1-3	Martin	15,798
30		10	(a)	Tottenham H	W 1-0	Cormack	21,697
31		13	(a)	Manchester U	L 0-2		40,473
32		20	(h)	Everton	W 3-2	Cormack 2, Storey-Moore	21,643
33		27	(h)	Crystal Palace	W 3-1	Storey-Moore 3 (1 pen)	16,506
34		31	(a)	Derby Co	W 2-1	Richardson, Storey-Moore	34,857
35	Apr	3	(a)	Wolverhampton W	L 0-4		20,531
36		9	(a)	Manchester C	W 3-1	McKenzie 2, Jackson	31,000
37		10	(h)	West Ham U	W 1-0	Storey-Moore	23,022
38		13	(h)	Arsenal	L 0-3		40,727
39		17	(a)	Blackpool	W 3-2	Cormack, Hindley, Storey-Moore	10,028
40		24	(h)	Liverpool	L 0-1		20,678
41		27	(h)	Stoke C	D 0-0		13,503
42	May	1	(a)	Leeds U	L 0-2		43,083

FINAL LEAGUE POSITION : 16th in Division One

Appearances

Sub. Appearances

Goals

Barron	Hindley	Winfield	Chapman	O'Kane	Newton	Lyons	Rees	Ingram	Cormack	Storey-Moore	Hilley	Richardson	McKenzie	Collier	Robertson	Jackson	McIntosh	Cottam	Fraser	Martin	
1	2	3	4	5	6	7	8	9*	10	11	12										1
1	2	3	4	5	6	7	8	9*	10	11	12										2
1	2	3	4	5	6	7	8	9	10	11		12									3
1	2	3	4	5	6	7	8	9	10	11											4
1	2	3	4	5	6	7	8	9	10	11*	12										5
1	2	3	4	5	6	7	8	9	10	11*		12									6
1	2	3	4	5	6	7	8	9	10	11											7
1	2	3	4	5	6	7	8	9*	10	11		12									8
1	2	3	4	5	6	7	8*		10	11	9	12									9
1	2	3	4	5	6	7	8	9	10		11*	12									10
1	2	3	4	5*	6	7	11	9	10			12	8								11
1	2	3	4	5	6	7	11	9	10			8*		12							12
1	2	3	4	5		7	11	9	10			8		12	6*						13
1	2	3	4	5		7	11		10			8	9			6					14
1	2	3	4	5		7	11		10			8	9			6					15
1	2	3	4	5			11*		10			8	9			6	7	12			16
1	2	3	4	5		7	11		10			8	9			6					17
1	2	3*	4	5	12	7			10	11		8	9			6					18
1	2	3	4	5		7			10	11		8	9			6					19
1	2*	3	4	5		7			10	11		8	9			6		12			20
1	2	3	4	5		7			10	11		8*	9			6			12		21
1	2	3	4	5					10	11		8	9			6	7				22
1	2	3	4	5		7			10	11		8	9			6					23
1	2	3	4	5		7			10	11			9			6			8		24
1	2	3	4	5		7			10	11			9			6			8		25
1	2	3	4	5		7*			10	11			9			6		12	8		26
1	2	3	4	5		7*			10	11						6		12	8	9	27
1	2	3	4	5		7			10	11						6			8	9	28
1	2	3	4	5		7			10	11						6			8	9	29
1	2	3	4	5		7			10	11		8				6				9	30
1	2	3	4	5		7	12		10	11		8				6				9*	31
1	2	3	4	5		7	12		10	11*		8				6				9	32
1	2	3	4	5		7			10	11		8				6				9	33
1	2	3	4	5		7	12		10	11		8*				6				9	34
1	2	3	4	5		7	12		10	11		8*				6				9	35
1	2	3	4	5					10	11		8		7					6	9	36
1	2	3	4	5					10	11		8		7					6	9	37
1	2	3	4	5		7	12		10	11		8							6	9*	38
1	2	3	4	5*			12		10	11		8	9	7					6		39
1	2	3	4	5			12		10	11		8	9	7*					6		40
1	2	3	4	5			12		10	11		8	9	7*					6		41
1	2	3	4	5			12		10	11*		8	9	7					6		42
42	42	42	42	42	12	33	26	12	41	33	2	25	5	7	1	22	2		19	12	
						1	9					3	4	3	2	1		1	2		
	2		1		1	3	3		8	18		1	2	1		1			1		

1971-72

#	Month	Date		Opponent	Res	Score	Scorers	Attendance
1	Aug	14	(a)	Liverpool	L	1-3	Storey-Moore (pen)	50,989
2		18	(a)	Leicester C	L	1-2	Cormack	32,079
3		21	(h)	West Ham U	W	1-0	Storey-Moore (pen)	17,185
4		24	(h)	Southampton	L	2-3	Martin, Storey-Moore	14,350
5		28	(a)	Crystal Palace	D	1-1	McKenzie	17,699
6		31	(h)	Stoke C	D	0-0		19,017
7	Sep	4	(h)	Sheffield U	L	2-3	Storey-Moore, Martin	27,041
8		11	(a)	Coventry C	D	1-1	Cormack	20,200
9		18	(h)	Manchester C	D	2-2	McKenzie, Storey-Moore (pen)	21,488
10		25	(a)	Wolverhampton W	L	2-4	Storey-Moore, Martin	20,631
11	Oct	2	(h)	Huddersfield T	L	1-2	McKenzie	15,693
12		9	(a)	Ipswich T	D	1-1	Storey-Moore	16,306
13		16	(h)	Liverpool	L	2-3	Storey-Moore 2	20,945
14		23	(a)	Tottenham H	L	1-6	Richardson	35,746
15		26	(a)	Huddersfield T	W	1-0	Lyons	9,459
16		30	(h)	Derby Co	L	0-2		37,710
17	Nov	6	(a)	Chelsea	L	0-2		25,812
18		13	(h)	West Brom A	W	4-1	Richardson, O'Neill, McKenzie, Storey-Moore	20,024
19		20	(a)	Newcastle U	L	1-2	Cormack	22,800
20		27	(h)	Leeds U	L	0-2		29,463
21	Dec	4	(a)	Manchester U	L	2-3	Cormack, O'Neill	45,411
22		11	(h)	Everton	W	1-0	Jackson	18,639
23		18	(a)	Sheffield U	L	1-2	Martin	27,663
24		27	(h)	Arsenal	D	1-1	Storey-Moore	42,750
25	Jan	1	(a)	Manchester C	D	2-2	Richardson, Martin	38,777
26		8	(h)	Crystal Palace	L	0-1		19,033
27		22	(h)	Leicester C	L	1-2	Storey-Moore	27,250
28		29	(a)	Southampton	L	1-4	Storey-Moore	15,043
29	Feb	12	(h)	Tottenham H	L	0-1		20,209
30		19	(a)	Derby Co	L	0-4		31,801
31	Mar	4	(a)	West Brom A	L	0-1		16,844
32		11	(h)	Ipswich T	L	0-2		9,872
33		14	(h)	Chelsea	W	2-1	Gemmell 2 (1 pen)	13,346
34		18	(a)	West Ham U	L	2-4	McKenzie 2	20,960
35		25	(h)	Coventry C	W	4-0	Gemmell, McKenzie, Richardson 2	12,205
36		27	(a)	Leeds U	L	1-6	Cormack	40,866
37	Apr	1	(a)	Arsenal	L	0-3		33,895
38		8	(h)	Newcastle U	W	1-0	Cormack	12,470
39		10	(a)	Stoke C	W	2-0	Gemmell, McIntosh	13,920
40		22	(h)	Manchester U	D	0-0		35,063
41		25	(h)	Wolverhampton W	L	1-3	Gemmell	16,889
42	May	2	(a)	Everton	D	1-1	Cormack	21,513

FINAL LEAGUE POSITION : 21st in Division One

Appearances

Sub. Appearances

Goals

16

Barron	Hindley	Winfield	Chapman	O'Kane	Fraser	Rees	Richardson	Martin	Cormack	Storey-Moore	Jackson	McKenzie	Lyons	Robertson	Hulme	Buckley	McIntosh	O'Neill	Cottam	Gemmell	Serella	
1	2	3	4	5	6	7	8	9	10	11												1
1	2	3	4	5*	6	7		9	10	11	12	8										2
1	2	3	4	5	6	7		9	10	11		8										3
1	2	3	4	5	6	7		9	10*	11	12	8										4
1	2	3	4	5	6	7		9	10	11		8										5
1	2	3	4	5	6	7			9	11	10	8										6
1	2	3	4	5	6	7		9	10*	11	12	8										7
1	2	3	4	5	6		12	9*	10	11	7	8										8
1	2	3	4	5	6			9	10	11	7	8										9
1	2	3	4	5	6			9	10*	11	7	8	12									10
1	2	3	4	5	6		12	9		11	10	8*	7									11
1	2	3	4	5			6	9		11	10	8	7									12
	2	3	4	5			6	9		11	10*	8	7	12	1							13
	2		4	5	3		6	9*		11		8	7	10	1	12						14
	5		4	2	3		6			11		8	7	10	1	9						15
	5		4	2	3		6			11		8	7	10	1	9						16
	5		4	2	3		6			11		8	7*	10	1	9	12					17
1	5		4	2	3		6		9	11		8	7	10*			12					18
1	5		4	2	3		6	12	9	11		8*	7					10				19
1	5		4	2	3		6	12	9	11			7*	8				10				20
1	5		4	2	3		6	10*	9	11			7	8				12				21
1	5		4	2*	3		6	9	10	11	7	12						8				22
1		3	4		2		6	9	10	11	7							8	5			23
1	5		4		2		6	9	10	11	7							8		3		24
1	5		4		2		6	9	10	11	8		7							3		25
1	5		4		2		6	9*		11	8	10	7					12		3		26
1	5		4		2		10	9		11		8				7			6	3		27
1	5		4		2		10	9*		11	12	8				7			6	3		28
1	5		4		2		10	9		11		8				7*	12		6	3		29
1	5	3	4				10	9		11			7					8	6	2		30
1	2		4		6		10	9		11			7					8	5	3		31
1		3	4		6		10	9*		11			7				12	8	5	2		32
1	2		4		6		10			11			7			9		8	5	3		33
1	2		4		6		10			11			7			9	12	8*	5	3		34
1	2						10		8	11		6				9	7		5	3	4	35
1	2						10		8	11		6				9	7		5	3	4	36
1	2						10		8	11		6*				9	7	12	5	3	4	37
1	2				6		10		8	11						9	7		5	3	4	38
1	2				6		10	9	8	11							7		5	3	4	39
1	2				6		10	9	8	11							7		5	3	4	40
1	2				6*		10	9	8	11							7	12	5	3	4	41
1	2	3			6		10	9	8	11							7*	12	5		4	42
37	40	17	34	22	36	7	32	23	32	30	12	31	19	12	5	9	11	10	17	18	8	
							2	2				3	2	1	1		1	3	7			
							5	5	7	13	1	7	1			1	2		5			

17

1972-73

1	Aug	12	(h)	Portsmouth	D	0-0		13,175
2		19	(a)	Hull C	D	0-0		11,189
3		26	(h)	Oxford U	W	2-1	Lyall, O'Neill	9,591
4		29	(h)	Brighton & HA	W	1-0	O'Neill	10,657
5	Sep	2	(a)	Carlisle U	W	2-1	McKenzie 2	7,626
6		9	(h)	Luton T	L	0-1		9,495
7		16	(a)	QPR	L	0-3		12,528
8		19	(h)	Cardiff C	W	2-1	O'Neill, Richardson	6,414
9		23	(h)	Aston Villa	D	1-1	Fraser	18,082
10		25	(a)	Millwall	L	1-2	Lyall	9,011
11		30	(a)	Sunderland	L	1-4	Richardson	14,155
12	Oct	7	(h)	Huddersfield T	D	1-1	Chapman	7,931
13		14	(a)	Bristol C	D	1-1	Fraser	13,861
14		21	(h)	Swindon T	D	2-2	Robertson, O'Neill	8,683
15		28	(a)	Sheffield W	W	2-1	Martin, Richardson	21,887
16	Nov	4	(h)	Millwall	W	3-2	Buckley, Gemmell (pen), Robertson	11,165
17		11	(a)	Cardiff C	L	1-2	Martin	12,750
18		18	(h)	Preston NE	L	0-1		10,383
19		25	(a)	Burnley	L	0-1		12,048
20	Dec	2	(h)	Orient	W	2-1	Lyall 2	7,959
21		9	(a)	Middlesbrough	D	0-0		10,326
22		16	(a)	Fulham	L	1-3	Galley	8,255
23		23	(h)	Blackpool	W	4-0	Martin, McKenzie, Fraser, Galley	10,078
24		26	(a)	Aston Villa	D	2-2	Galley, Martin	37,000
25	Jan	6	(a)	Oxford U	L	0-1		8,836
26		20	(h)	Carlisle U	W	2-1	Martin, Robertson (pen)	6,866
27		27	(a)	Luton T	L	0-1		10,983
28	Feb	10	(h)	QPR	D	0-0		11,617
29		17	(a)	Portsmouth	L	0-2		11,151
30		24	(h)	Fulham	W	2-1	Galley, McIntosh	8,810
31	Mar	3	(a)	Huddersfield T	D	1-1	Hindley	7,473
32		10	(h)	Bristol C	W	1-0	Galley	8,860
33		13	(h)	Hull C	L	1-2	Robertson (pen)	7,711
34		17	(a)	Swindon T	D	0-0		9,842
35		24	(h)	Sheffield W	W	3-0	Galley, O'Neill, Cottam	10,488
36		31	(h)	Burnley	W	3-0	McKenzie, O'Neill, Lyons	12,522
37	Apr	7	(a)	Orient	L	0-3		6,373
38		14	(h)	Middlesbrough	L	1-3	McKenzie	9,258
39		21	(a)	Preston NE	L	1-2	Hindley	7,701
40		23	(a)	Blackpool	L	0-2		8,322
41		24	(h)	Sunderland	W	1-0	Martin	10,306
42		28	(a)	Brighton & HA	D	2-2	Dennehy, McKenzie	9,706

FINAL LEAGUE POSITION : 14th in Division Two

Appearances

Sub. Appearances

Goals

Barron	Fraser	Gemmell	Serella	Chapman	Robertson	McIntosh	Lyall	McKenzie	Richardson	O'Neill	Hindley	Buckley	Cottam	Lyons	Martin	Winfield	Galley	Jackson	O'Kane	Baines	Dennehy	Peacock	
1	2	3	4	5	6	7	8	9	10	11													1
1	6	3	4	5		7	8	9	10	11	2												2
1	6	3	4	5		7*	8	9	10	11	2	12											3
1	6	3	4	5		7	8	9	10	11	2												4
1	6	3	4			7	8	9	10	11	2		5										5
1	6	3	4		10	7	8	9		11	2		5										6
1	6	3	4		12		8*	9	10	11	2		5	7									7
1	6	3	4				8	9	10	11	2		5	7									8
1	6	3	4	12		7	8*	9	10	11	2		5										9
1	6	3	4	12		7*	8	9	10	11	2		5										10
1	6	3	4	8	12		7*	9	10	11	2		5										11
1	6	3	4	9	8*		7		10	12	2	11	5										12
1	6	3	4	9	8		7		10		2	11	5										13
1	6	3	4	9	8		7		10*	12	2	11	5										14
1	6	3	5	4	10			8		12	2	11			7*	9							15
1	6	3	5	4	10*		8			12	2	11			7	9							16
1	6	3	5*	4	10		8			12	2	11			7	9							17
1	6	3	5	4	10		8			12	2	11*			7	9							18
1	6*	3	5	4	10		8	11	12	7	2					9							19
1			5	4	10	8	11	6	7		2					9	3						20
1			5	4	10	12	8	11*	6	7	2				9		3						21
1			5	4	10	12	11	6	7*		2				8		3	9					22
1	6*		5	4	8		11			7	2				9		3	10	12				23
1	6	2			8	7	11			4		5			9		3	10					24
1	6	2	4	8			11	12	7*	5					9		3	10					25
1	6	5	4	8	7*	12			11	2					9		3	10					26
1	6	5*	4	8	7	12			11	2					9		3	10					27
1	6	5	4		7	8			11	2					9		3	10					28
1	6	5	4	8	7	11				2					9		3	10					29
1	6	5	4	8	7	11				2					9		3	10					30
1	6	5	4	8	7	11				2					9		3	10					31
1	6	5	4	8	7	11		9		2							3	10					32
1	6	5*	4	8	7	11		12							9		3	10	2				33
1			4	7		9	8		5	11					3		10	6	2				34
1			4	12	7	9	8*		5	11					3		10	6	2				35
1			4	7		9	8		5	11					3		10	6	2				36
1			4	8	7	9			5	11					3		10	6	2				37
1			4	12	7	9	8		5	11					3		10	6	2*				38
1			6	7		10	8	2	5						3	9			4	11			39
1		5	6	7		9	11	2		8					3		10		4				40
1		5	6	7	10	8	2		4	9	3							11					41
		5	8	6	7	10	2		4	9	3							11	1				42
41	30	21	34	32	28	23	26	27	20	31	35	7	19	10	19	23	18	6	6	2	3	1	
			2	4	1	5	1	2	4		1						1						
	3	1		1	4	1	4	6	3	6	2	1	1	1	6		6			1			

1973-74

1	Aug	25	(h)	Luton T	W	4-0	Jackson 2 (1 pen), Martin, McKenzie	10,793
2	Sep	1	(a)	Oxford U	L	0-1		7,638
3		8	(h)	Sheffield W	W	2-1	McKenzie 2	13,452
4		11	(a)	Hull C	D	0-0		8,134
5		15	(a)	West Brom A	D	3-3	McKenzie 2, Martin	14,895
6		18	(h)	Swindon T	W	2-0	McKenzie 2	11,031
7		22	(h)	Preston NE	D	1-1	O'Neill	12,958
8		29	(a)	Bolton W	L	0-1		15,101
9	Oct	2	(a)	Swindon T	D	0-0		6,353
10		6	(h)	Millwall	W	3-0	McKenzie 2, Lyall	11,311
11		13	(a)	Orient	L	1-2	Lyall	8,346
12		20	(a)	Blackpool	D	2-2	McKenzie, Bowyer	8,101
13		23	(h)	Hull C	D	0-0		10,392
14		27	(h)	Aston Villa	L	1-2	McKenzie	17,718
15	Nov	3	(a)	Crystal Palace	W	1-0	McKenzie	21,881
16		10	(h)	Fulham	W	3-0	Jackson, Bowyer, Martin	10,530
17		17	(h)	Carlisle U	W	2-0	Martin, McKenzie	11,153
18		24	(a)	Sunderland	D	0-0		22,252
19	Dec	8	(a)	Cardiff C	D	1-1	Lyall (pen)	10,339
20		15	(a)	Middlesbrough	L	0-1		16,764
21		22	(h)	Bolton W	W	3-2	Bowyer 2, Cottam	9,498
22		26	(a)	Notts Co	W	1-0	Lyall (pen)	30,036
23		29	(a)	Sheffield W	D	1-1	McKenzie	16,332
24	Jan	1	(h)	Oxford U	D	1-1	Bowyer	15,079
25		12	(h)	West Brom A	L	1-4	McKenzie	15,501
26		19	(a)	Luton T	D	2-2	McKenzie, Richardson	11,888
27	Feb	2	(h)	Middlesbrough	W	5-1	Lyall 2, Bowyer, Winfield, Martin	16,764
28		10	(a)	Preston NE	L	1-2	McKenzie	13,486
29		23	(a)	Millwall	D	0-0		8,763
30		26	(h)	Orient	W	2-1	Martin, Lyall	16,632
31	Mar	3	(h)	Notts Co	D	0-0		29,657
32		16	(h)	Blackpool	W	2-0	McKenzie 2	15,724
33		23	(a)	Fulham	L	0-2		8,884
34		26	(h)	Portsmouth	W	2-0	Lyall 2	14,040
35		30	(h)	Crystal Palace	L	1-2	Lyall (pen)	16,330
36	Apr	6	(h)	Sunderland	D	2-2	Richardson, McKenzie	18,044
37		12	(a)	Bristol C	L	0-1		13,125
38		13	(a)	Carlisle U	L	1-2	McKenzie	9,258
39		16	(h)	Bristol C	D	1-1	McKenzie	12,756
40		20	(h)	Cardiff C	W	2-1	Lyall, McKenzie	11,138
41		24	(a)	Aston Villa	L	1-3	McKenzie	12,439
42		27	(a)	Portsmouth	W	2-0	McKenzie 2	11,765

FINAL LEAGUE POSITION : 7th in Division Two

Appearances
Sub. Appearances
Goals

Football appearances and shirt-number grid (page 21). Columns are players; the right-hand column is the match number (1–42).

Barron	O'Kane	Winfield	Serella	Cottam	Jackson	McKenzie	O'Neill	Martin	Lyall	Dennehy	Galley	Chapman	Richardson	Hindley	Peplow	Bowyer	Peacock	Robertson	McIntosh	Woodcock	No.
1	2	3	4	5	6	7	8	9	10	11											1
1	2	3	4	5	6*	7	8	9	10	11	12										2
1	2	3		5		7	8*	9	6	11	10	4	12								3
1	2	3		5		7	8	9	6	11		4		10							4
1	2	3		5		7	8	9	6	11		4	12	10*							5
1	2	3		5		7	8	9*	6	11	12	4		10							6
1	2	3		5		7	8	9	6	11*	12	4		10							7
1	2*	3		5	12	7	8	9	6	11		4		10							8
1	2	3		5	11	7	8		6		9	4		10							9
1	2	3		5	8	10	7		6		11	4		9							10
1	2	3		5		7	8	9	6	12	11*	4		10							11
1*	2	3		5	10	7	8	9	6		12	4				11					12
	2	3		5	10	7	8	9	6			4				11	1				13
1	2	3		5	10	7	8	9	6*			4	12			11					14
1	2	3		5	10	7	8	9	6			4				11					15
1	2	3		5	6	7	10	9	8			4				11					16
1	2		3	5		7		9	6		8	4				11		10			17
1	2		3	5			8	9	6		10	4				11		7			18
1	2	3		5		11	12	8	6			4	10			9	7*				19
1	2	3		5		7	10	9	8			4	6			11					20
1	2	3		5		7	10	9	6			4	8			11					21
1	2	3	4			7	10	9	8			6	5			11					22
1	2	3		5	12	7	10	9	8		6*	4				11					23
1	2	3		5		7	10	8	9		6	4				11					24
1	2	3*		5		7	10	9	8	12	6	4				11					25
1	2	3	12	5	10	8	9	7				4	6*			11					26
1	2	3		5	6	8	9	7				4	10			11					27
1	2	3		5	10	7		9	8			4	6			11					28
1	2	3	5			7	10	8	9			4	6			11					29
1	2	3	5			10	7	9	8			4	6			11					30
1	2	3	5			10	7	9	8			4				11			6		31
1	2	3	5			7		9	8			4	6			11			10		32
1	2	3	5		10*	7	12	9	8			4	6			11					33
1	2	3		5		7		9	8			4	6			11			10		34
1	2	3	5			7		9	8			4	6			11			10		35
1	2	3	5			7		9	8		12	4	6			11			10*		36
	2	3		5		7		9	8	12	10	4	6*			11	1				37
	2	3	6	5		7		9	8	11*		4	10				1	12			38
	2	3		5	6	7	8	9				4				11	1			10	39
	2	3		5		7		9	8		10	4	6				1	11			40
	2	3	5			7	11	8	9			4	6				1	10			41
	2	2	5		10	7		9	8			4	6				1			11	42
35	42	38	15	34	19	41	25	36	41	8	10	38	22	8	3	28	7	5	5	2	
		1		2		2				3	5		3				1				
	1		1	3	26	1		6	11				2			6					

21

1974-75

#	Month	Date	Venue	Opponent	Result	Score	Scorers	Attendance
1	Aug	17	(h)	Bristol C	D	0-0		11,339
2		19	(a)	Millwall	L	0-3		7,509
3		24	(a)	Portsmouth	L	0-2		11,340
4		27	(h)	Millwall	W	2-1	Martin, Bowyer	7,957
5		31	(h)	Oxford U	L	1-2	Bowyer	9,257
6	Sep	7	(a)	Manchester C	D	2-2	Bowyer, Cottam	40,671
7		14	(h)	Hull C	W	4-0	Martin 2, Lyall, O'Neill	9,437
8		17	(h)	Portsmouth	L	1-2	Jones	9,534
9		21	(a)	Sheffield W	W	3-2	Martin 2, Bowyer	15,295
10		28	(h)	Sunderland	D	1-1	Lyall (pen)	14,885
11	Oct	2	(a)	Aston Villa	L	0-3		20,357
12		5	(a)	Southampton	W	1-0	Jackson	15,703
13		12	(h)	Norwich C	L	1-3	Butlin	13,613
14		19	(a)	West Brom A	W	1-0	Richardson	13,518
15		26	(h)	Bristol R	W	1-0	Martin	11,495
16	Nov	2	(a)	Bolton W	L	0-2		12,396
17		9	(h)	Oldham Ath	W	1-0	Dennehy	10,127
18		16	(a)	Cardiff C	L	1-2	Martin	9,401
19		23	(h)	York C	W	2-1	Bowyer, Richardson	10,271
20		30	(a)	Orient	D	1-1	Bowyer	5,217
21	Dec	7	(h)	Fulham	D	1-1	Martin	10,057
22		14	(a)	Bristol C	L	0-1		10,006
23		21	(h)	Blackpool	D	0-0		8,480
24		26	(a)	Hull C	W	3-1	Martin 2, Butlin	12,278
25		28	(h)	Notts Co	L	0-2		25,013
26	Jan	11	(a)	Fulham	W	1-0	Butlin	9,159
27		18	(h)	Orient	D	2-2	Richardson 2	17,582
28	Feb	1	(a)	Oldham Ath	L	0-2		10,736
29		8	(h)	Bolton W	L	2-3	Dennehy 2	11,992
30		14	(a)	York C	D	1-1	Lyall	7,029
31		22	(h)	Cardiff C	D	0-0		12,806
32		28	(a)	Oxford U	D	1-1	Lyall	7,390
33	Mar	8	(h)	Aston Villa	L	2-3	O'Hare, Butlin	20,205
34		15	(a)	Sunderland	D	0-0		30,812
35		22	(h)	Manchester U	L	0-1		21,893
36		25	(a)	Notts Co	D	2-2	Lyall, Butlin	20,303
37		29	(a)	Blackpool	D	0-0		11,640
38	Apr	1	(h)	Sheffield W	W	1-0	Lyall (pen)	14,077
39		5	(a)	Bristol R	L	2-4	Lyall, O'Hare	9,684
40		12	(h)	Southampton	D	0-0		11,554
41		19	(a)	Norwich C	L	0-3		24,552
42		26	(h)	West Brom A	W	2-1	Butlin 2	11,721

FINAL LEAGUE POSITION : 16th in Division Two

Appearances

Sub. Appearaces

Goals

22

Football appearances and goals grid (shirt numbers by match). Columns are players (left to right); the final column is the match number (1–42).

Peacock	O'Kane	Richardson	Chapman	Cottam	Jones	Dennehy	Lyall	Martin	Robertson	Bowyer	Woodcock	Galley	Serella	Jackson	O'Neill	Anderson	Butlin	Greenwood	Middleton	McIntosh	McGovern	O'Hare	McCann	#
1	2	3	4	5	6	7	8	9*	10	11	12													1
1	2	6	4	5	3	7	8		10	12	11	9*												2
1	2	6	4	5	3*	7	8		10	9	12		11											3
1	2	6	4	5	3	7	8	10		12		9*	11											4
1	2	6	4		3	11	8	9		10		12	5	7*										5
1	2	6	4	5	3	7	8	9*		10		12			11									6
1	2	6	4	5	3	7	8	9	12	10*					11									7
1	2		4	5	3	7	8	9	6	10					12	11*								8
1	4				3	7	8	9	10				5	6	11	2								9
1	4	6			3	7	8	9	10				5		11	2								10
1	4	6			3	7	8		10				5		11	2	9							11
1	2	6	4	5	7		8		10						11		9	3						12
1	2	6	4		3	7	12	9*	8						11		10	5						13
	2	6	4	5	7	11	8		10*						12		9	3	1					14
	2	6*		5	7	10	8				12		4		11		9	3	1					15
1	2	6		5	11		8	9*					4	7	12		10	3						16
	2		4	5	7	8	9		6						11		10	3	1					17
	2	12	4	5	7	8	9		6						11		10	3*	1					18
	2	6	4	5	11		8	9	10						7*		12	3	1					19
	2	6	4	12	5		11	9*	10						7		8	3	1					20
	2	11	4	5	7		8		10		12				6*		9	3	1					21
	2	6	4	5	7			9*	12	10					11		8	3	1					22
	2	6	4	5	7	8			10						11		9	3*	1	12				23
	3	6	4	5		11	8		10							2	9		1		7			24
	3	6	4	5	12	11		9	10							2	8		1		7*			25
	2	6	4	5	7	8			10						11		9	3	1					26
	2	6	4	5	7	8			10						11		9	3	1					27
	2		4	5		7		9	6	10					11		8	3	1					28
			4	5	3	11	7		6	10						2	8	9						29
	2	3	4	5	7			9						6	10	11	8		1					30
	5	4	3		7		9	8	10						11	2			1		6			31
	4	3		5	7		8								11	2	10		1		6	9		32
	3	6		5	7		8*							11	12	2	10		1		4	9		33
	3	8		5	7								4		11	2	10		1		6	9		34
	5	3	6	8	7										11	2	10		1		4	9		35
	4	3	8	5	7		12							6	11	2*	10		1			9		36
	2	3	4	5		8								6	11	7	10		1			9		37
	4	3	8	5	7									6	11	2	10		1			9		38
	2	3	6	5	7		8								11		10		1		4	9		39
	2	3	4	5		11	7							6			10		1		8	9		40
	2	3	4	5	7*		8							6	12		10		1		11	9		41
	3	6*	4	5			12								11	2	10	8	1			7	9	42
14	41	37	31	14	36	26	36	26	17	30	5	3	8	14	16	14	29	15	28	3	8	10	1	
	1		1		1	1	1	3	2	4		1	2	2		2	1				1			
	4		1	1	3	7	10			6			1	1			7		2					

23

1975-76

1	Aug	16	(h)	Plymouth A	W 2-0	Horswill (og), O'Hare	13,083
2		23	(a)	Portsmouth	D 1-1	Bowyer	10,655
3		30	(h)	Notts Co	L 0-1		19,757
4	Sep	6	(a)	Chelsea	D 0-0		21,023
5		13	(h)	Hull C	L 1-2	Robertson	12,191
6		20	(a)	Oxford U	W 1-0	Lyall	5,068
7		24	(h)	Charlton Ath	L 1-2	Robertson	10,588
8		27	(h)	Bolton W	L 1-2	Lyall	10,775
9	Oct	4	(a)	Bristol R	L 2-4	Robertson, Bowyer	7,689
10		11	(a)	Fulham	D 0-0		10,149
11		18	(h)	Southampton	W 3-1	O'Neill, O'Hare, Cottam	12,677
12		21	(h)	Luton T	D 0-0		12,290
13		25	(a)	Oldham Ath	D 0-0		11,324
14	Nov	1	(h)	Carlisle U	W 4-0	Butlin, O'Hare 2, Curran (pen)	11,894
15		4	(a)	Blackpool	D 1-1	O'Neill	5,851
16		8	(a)	Sunderland	L 0-3		31,227
17		15	(h)	Bristol C	W 1-0	Butlin	11,583
18		22	(a)	Southampton	W 3-0	Bowyer 2, Richardson	14,245
19		29	(h)	York C	W 1-0	Butlin	13,108
20	Dec	6	(a)	Orient	D 1-1	Bowyer	5,629
21		13	(h)	Portsmouth	L 0-1		11,343
22		20	(a)	Plymouth A	L 0-1		10,545
23		26	(h)	West Brom A	L 0-2		19,395
24		27	(a)	Blackburn R	W 4-1	Bowery 2, Robertson, Bowyer	10,724
25	Jan	10	(a)	Hull C	L 0-1		6,465
26		17	(h)	Chelsea	L 1-3	Bowyer	14,172
27		31	(a)	Luton T	D 1-1	Curran	8,503
28	Feb	7	(h)	Blackpool	W 3-0	Curran, Butlin, Bowyer	8,582
29		21	(a)	Bristol C	W 2-0	Curran, O'Hare	15,302
30		24	(a)	Charlton Ath	D 2-2	Bowyer, McCann	10,655
31		28	(h)	Oldham Ath	W 4-3	Butlin, O'Neill 2, Curran (pen)	11,509
32	Mar	6	(a)	Carlisle U	D 1-1	Barry (og)	7,153
33		13	(h)	Fulham	W 1-0	O'Hare	11,445
34		17	(h)	Sunderland	W 2-1	Bowyer, O'Hare	16,995
35		20	(a)	York C	L 2-3	O'Hare, Downing (og)	5,571
36		27	(h)	Orient	W 1-0	Bowyer	11,127
37	Apr	3	(a)	Bolton W	D 0-0		21,464
38		10	(h)	Oxford U	W 4-0	Butlin, O'Neill, Curran (pen), Robertson	11,259
39		13	(a)	Notts Co	D 0-0		28,766
40		17	(a)	West Brom A	L 0-2		26,447
41		20	(h)	Blackburn R	W 1-0	Butlin	13,006
42		24	(h)	Bristol R	W 3-0	O'Hare, Bowyer 2	12,127

FINAL LEAGUE POSITION : 7th in Division Two

Appearances

Sub. Appearances

Goals

Middleton	Anderson	Clark	Chapman	O'Kane	McGovern	Lyall	Richardson	O'Hare	Robertson	Bowyer	O'Neill	Gunn	Curran	Cottam	Sunley	Butlin	Wells	McIntosh	Bowery	McCann	Barrett	No.
1	2	3	4	5	6	7	8	9	10	11												1
1	2	3	5	4*	8	11	6	9	7	10	12											2
1	2	4	5		8		6	9	10	11		3	7									3
1	2	5	4		8		10	9	6	11		3	7									4
1	2	6	5	4			8	9	10	11		3	7									5
1	2	4	5		8	12	6	9	10	11*		3	7									6
1	2	4	5		8		10	6		11	9	3	7									7
1		3	6		4		10	8		11	9	2	7	5								8
1		3	5		4	12	8	9	10	11		2	7*	6								9
1	2	3	4		8		10	6	12	11			7*	5	9							10
1	2	3			4		6	9		11	8		7	5		10						11
1	2	3			4		6	9	11		8		7	5		10						12
1	2	3			4		6	9		11	8		7	5		10						13
1	2	3			4		6*	9	12	11	8		7	5		10						14
1	2	3			4		6	9	7	11	8			5		10						15
1	2	3	5		4		6	9	8	11	7					10						16
1	2	3	5		4		6	9	8	11	7					10						17
1	2	3	5		4		6	9	8	11	7					10						18
	2	3	5		4		6	9	8	11	7					10	1					19
	2	3	5		4			9	6	11	8		7			10	1					20
	2	3	5		4			9	6	11	8		7			10	1					21
	2	3	5		4		6	9	12	11	8		7*			10	1					22
		3	5	2	4		6	9		11	8					10	1					23
		3	5	2	4			9	6	11						10	1	7	8			24
	2*	3	5		4		6	9	8	11	7					10	1		12			25
		4	5	2			6	9	11		8	3	7			10	1					26
		3	5	2	4			9	11	6	8		7			10	1					27
		3	5	2	4			9	11	6	8		7			10	1					28
		3	5	2*	4			10	11	6	8		7			9	1		12			29
		3	5		4			9	11	6	8	2	7			10*	1		12			30
		3	5		4			9	11	6	8	2	7			10	1					31
1		3	5		4			9	11	6		2	7			10				8		32
		3	2		4			9	11	6	8		7			10	1			5		33
		3	5		4			9	11	6	8		7			10	1				2	34
		3	5		4			9	11	6	8		7			10*	1		12		2	35
		3	5		4			9	11	6	8	7*				10	1		12		2	36
		3	5		4			9	11	6	8		7			10	1				2	37
		3	5		4			9	11	6	8		7			10	1				2	38
		3	5		4			9	11	6	8		7			10	1				2	39
		3	5		4		12	9	11*	6	8		7			10	1				2	40
		3	5		4			9	11	6	8		7			10	1				2	41
		3	5		4			9	11	6	8		7			10	1				2	42
19	21	42	37	8	41	5	23	39	37	40	29	11	33	8	1	32	23	1	1	1	10	
						2	1	1	2		1						1		4			
						2	1	9	5	13	5		6	1		7			2	1		

1976-77

1	Aug	21	(a)	Fulham	D	2-2	Curran, O'Hare	9,437
2		25	(h)	Charlton Ath	D	1-1	Curran (pen)	12,662
3		28	(h)	Wolverhampton W	L	1-3	Daley (og)	17,222
4	Sep	4	(a)	Luton T	D	1-1	Curran (pen)	11,231
5		11	(h)	Hereford U	W	4-3	Butlin, Bowyer 2, Robertson	12,081
6		18	(a)	Southampton	D	1-1	Bowyer	23,006
7		25	(h)	Carlisle U	W	5-1	O'Hare, Bowyer 2, Barret, Withe	12,479
8	Oct	2	(a)	Hull C	L	0-1		16,096
9		9	(h)	Sheffield U	W	6-1	Bowyer 2, Butlin, Curran, Withe, Anderson	17,801
10		16	(a)	Blackpool	L	0-1		17,089
11		23	(h)	Burnley	W	5-2	Curran, Robertson (pen), Butlin, O'Neill 2	15,281
12		30	(a)	Oldham Ath	L	0-1		10,597
13	Nov	6	(h)	Blackburn R	W	3-0	Bowyer, Withe, Haslegrave	12,972
14		13	(a)	Orient	W	1-0	Woodcock	5,921
15		20	(h)	Chelsea	D	1-1	O'Neill	27,089
16		27	(a)	Cardiff C	W	3-0	Withe, Chapman, Woodcock	12,770
17	Dec	4	(h)	Bristol R	W	4-2	Robertson 2 (1 pen), Woodcock, Withe	16,302
18		11	(a)	Millwall	W	2-0	O'Neill, O'Hare	9,307
19		18	(h)	Plymouth A	D	1-1	Barrett	15,180
20		27	(a)	Bolton W	D	1-1	Withe	31,313
21	Jan	1	(a)	Blackburn R	W	3-1	Withe, Bowyer, Woodcock	14,534
22		14	(a)	Charlton Ath	L	1-2	Bowyer	7,992
23		22	(h)	Fulham	W	3-0	Lloyd, O'Neill, Woodcock	24,718
24	Feb	5	(a)	Wolverhampton W	L	1-2	Chapman	30,661
25		12	(h)	Luton T	L	1-2	Lloyd	18,225
26	Mar	2	(a)	Hereford U	W	1-0	Curran	7,503
27		5	(a)	Carlisle U	D	1-1	Robertson (pen)	7,603
28		8	(h)	Notts Co	L	1-2	Withe	31,004
29		12	(h)	Hull C	W	2-0	Woodcock, Withe	15,125
30		19	(a)	Sheffield U	L	0-2		20,370
31		22	(h)	Southampton	W	2-1	Woodcock, O'Neill	12,393
32		26	(h)	Blackpool	W	3-0	Withe 2, Woodcock	16,658
33		29	(h)	Orient	W	3-0	Withe 2, Lloyd	16,267
34	Apr	2	(a)	Burnley	W	1-0	Woodcock	10,904
35		6	(h)	Bolton W	W	3-1	O'Neill, Withe, Bowyer	24,580
36		9	(a)	Notts Co	D	1-1	Withe	32,498
37		16	(a)	Chelsea	L	1-2	O'Neill	36,499
38		23	(h)	Cardiff C	L	0-1		20,646
39		27	(h)	Oldham Ath	W	3-0	Bowyer, Woodcock, O'Neill	17,139
40		30	(a)	Bristol R	D	1-1	Robertson	8,893
41	May	2	(a)	Plymouth A	W	2-1	Woodcock, Withe	13,542
42		7	(h)	Millwall	W	1-0	Moore (og)	23,529

FINAL LEAGUE POSITION : 3rd in Division Two   Appearances

Sub. Appearances

Goals

Wells	Saunders	Clark	McGovern	Chapman	Bowyer	Curran	Haslegrave	O'Hare	Butlin	Robertson	Richardson	O'Neill	Barrett	Middleton	Anderson	Withe	Lloyd	Woodcock	Bowery	Birtles	
1	2	3	4	5	6	7	8*	9	10	11	12										1
1	2	3	4	5	6	7		9	10	11	8*	12									2
1	2	3	4	5	11	7		9	10	8		12	6*								3
		3	4*	5	6	7		9	10	11		8	2	1	12						4
1		3	4*	5	6	7		9	10	11		8	2		12						5
		3		5	6	7		9	10	11		8	2	1	4						6
		3	4	5	6	7		9		11		8	2	1		10					7
		3	4		6	7	9*			11		8	2	1	12	10	5				8
		3	4		6	7			10	11		8		1	2	9	5				9
		3	4		6	7*	12		10	11		8		1	2	9	5				10
		3	4		6	7*			10	11		8	12	1	2	9	5				11
	2	3	5		6		12		10	11		8	7*	1	4	9					12
		3	5	4	6	7			10			8		1	2	9		11			13
		3	4	5	6	7				11		8		1	2	9		10			14
		3	4	5	6	7				11		8		1	2	9		10			15
		3	4	5	6			8		11		7		1	2	9		10			16
		3	4		6			8		11		7		1	2	9	5	10			17
		3	4		6	7				11		8		1	2	9	5	10			18
		3	6	10		7						8	4	1	2		5	11	9		19
		3	4		6	7				11		8		1	2	9	5	10			20
		3	4		6	7				11		8		1	2	9	5	10			21
		3	4		7	6				11		8		1	2	9	5	10			22
		3	4		6	7				11		8		1	2	9	5	10			23
		3	4	12	6	7				11		8*		1	2	9	5	10			24
		3	4	9	6	7		8		11				1	2		5	10			25
		3	5		6	7*	12			11		8	4	1	2	9		10			26
		3	4	5		7*		9		11		8	6	1	2	12		10			27
		3	4	5	6	7				11		8		1	2	9		10			28
		3	4	5	6					11		7		1	2	9		10		8	29
		3	6	4	8	12				11		7		1	2	9	5	10*			30
		3	7	4	6					11		8		1	2	9	5	10			31
		3	7	4	6					11		8		1	2	9	5	10			32
		3	7	4	6			12		11		8		1	2	9*	5	10			33
		3	7	4	6					11		8	12	1	2	9*	5	10			34
		3	7	4	6			12		11		8		1	2	9*	5	10			35
		3	7*	4	6					11		8	12	1	2	9	5	10			36
		3	7	4	6					11		8		1	2	9	5	10			37
		3	7	4	6			12		11		8		1	2	9*	5	10			38
		3*	7	4	6	12				11		8		1	2	9	5	10			39
		3	7	4*	6	12				11		8		1	2	9	5	10			40
		3	7	4	6					11		8		1	2	9	5	10			41
		3	7	4	6					11		8		1	2	9	5	10			42
4	4	42	39	31	41	13	5	19	10	41	1	38	10	38	35	33	26	30	1	1	
			1			2	2	3	2		1	2	3		3	1					
			2	12	6	1	3	3	6			9	2		1	16	3	11			

1977-78

1	Aug	20	(a)	Everton	W	3-1	Withe, Robertson, O'Neill	38,001
2		23	(h)	Bristol C	W	1-0	Withe	21,743
3		27	(h)	Derby Co	W	3-0	Withe 2, Robertson	28,807
4	Sep	3	(a)	Arsenal	L	0-3		40,810
5		10	(a)	Wolverhampton W	W	3-2	Withe, Bowyer, Woodcock	24,622
6		17	(h)	Aston Villa	W	2-0	Woodcock, Robertson	31,016
7		24	(a)	Leicester C	W	3-0	O'Neill, Woodcock, Robertson (pen)	21,447
8	Oct	1	(h)	Norwich C	D	1-1	Burns	23,741
9		4	(h)	Ipswich T	W	4-0	Withe 4	26,845
10		8	(a)	West Ham U	D	0-0		26,128
11		15	(h)	Manchester C	W	2-1	Woodcock, Withe	35,572
12		22	(a)	QPR	W	2-0	Bowyer, Burns	24,248
13		29	(h)	Middlesbrough	W	4-0	Anderson 2, Bowyer, McGovern	27,373
14	Nov	5	(a)	Chelsea	L	0-1		36,116
15		12	(h)	Manchester U	W	2-1	Burns, Gemmill	30,183
16		19	(a)	Leeds U	L	0-1		42,925
17		26	(h)	West Brom A	D	0-0		31,908
18	Dec	3	(a)	Birmingham C	W	2-0	O'Neill, Woodcock	29,925
19		10	(h)	Coventry C	W	2-1	O'Neill, McGovern	29,823
20		17	(a)	Manchester U	W	4-0	Greenhoff (og), Woodcock 2, Robertson	54,375
21		26	(h)	Liverpool	D	1-1	Gemmill	47,218
22		28	(a)	Newcastle U	W	2-0	Needham, McGovern	40,735
23		31	(a)	Bristol C	W	3-1	Needham, Woodcock, O'Neill	31,990
24	Jan	2	(h)	Everton	D	1-1	Robertson (pen)	44,030
25		14	(a)	Derby Co	D	0-0		36,500
26		21	(h)	Arsenal	W	2-0	Needham, Gemmill	35,743
27	Feb	4	(a)	Wolverhampton W	W	2-0	Woodcock, McGovern	28,803
28		25	(a)	Norwich C	D	3-3	Withe, Barrett, O'Neill	26,004
29	Mar	4	(h)	West Ham U	W	2-0	Needham, Robertson (pen)	33,924
30		14	(h)	Leicester C	W	1-0	Robertson (pen)	32,355
31		25	(h)	Newcastle U	W	2-0	Robertson (pen), Anderson	35,552
32		29	(a)	Middlesbrough	D	2-2	Woodcock, O'Neill	25,445
33	Apr	1	(h)	Chelsea	W	3-1	Burns, O'Neill, Robertson	31,262
34		5	(a)	Aston Villa	W	1-0	Woodcock	44,215
35		11	(a)	Manchester C	D	0-0		43,428
36		15	(h)	Leeds U	D	1-1	Withe	38,662
37		18	(h)	QPR	W	1-0	Robertson (pen)	30,339
38		22	(a)	Coventry C	D	0-0		36,881
39		25	(a)	Ipswich T	W	2-0	Mariner (og), Clark	30,062
40		29	(h)	Birmingham C	D	0-0		37,625
41	May	2	(a)	West Brom A	D	2-2	Robertson (pen), Bowyer	23,612
42		4	(a)	Liverpool	D	0-0		50,021

FINAL LEAGUE POSITION : 1st in Division One

Appearances

Sub. Appearances

Goals

Middleton	Anderson	Clark	McGovern	Lloyd	Burns	O'Neill	Bowyer	Withe	Woodcock	Robertson	Barrett	Shilton	O'Hare	Gemmill	Needham	No.
1	2	3	4	5	6	7	8	9	10	11						1
1	2	3	4	5	6	7	8	9	10	11						2
1	2	3	4	5	6	7	8	9	10	11						3
1	2	3*	4	5	6	7	8	9	10	11	12					4
1	2		4	5	6	7	8	9	10	11	3					5
	2		4	5	6	7	8	9	10	11	3	1				6
	2		4	5	6	7	8		10	11	3	1	9			7
	2			5	6	7	4	9	10	11	3	1		8		8
	2		4	5	6	7	8	9	10	11	3	1				9
	2		4	5	6	7	8*	9	10	11	3	1		12		10
	2		4	5	6	7*	8	9	10	11	3	1		12		11
	2			5	6	7	8	9	10	11	3	1		4		12
	2		4	5*	6	12	8	9	10	11	3	1		7		13
	2		4	5	6	12	8*	9	10	11	3	1		7		14
	2		4	5	6		8	9	10	11	3	1		7		15
	2		4	5	6		8	9	10	11	3	1		7		16
	2		4	5	6	8		9	10	11	3	1		7		17
	2		4	5	6	7		9	10	11	3	1		8		18
	2		4	5	6	7		9	10	11	3	1		8		19
	2		4		6	7		9	10	11	3	1		8	5	20
	2		4		6	7		9	10	11	3	1		8	5	21
	2		4		6	7	12	9*	10	11	3	1		8	5	22
	2		4		6	7		9	10	11	3	1		8	5	23
	2		4		6	7		9	10	11	3	1		8	5	24
	2		4		6	7		9	10	11	3	1		8	5	25
	2		4		6	7		9	10	11	3	1		8	5	26
	2		4		6	7		9	10	11	3	1		8	5	27
	2		4		6	7		9	10	11	3	1		8	5	28
		3			6	7	2	9	10	11		1	4	8	5	29
	2	3			6	7		9	10	11		1	4	8	5	30
	2*	3			6	7	12	9	10	11		1	4	8	5	31
		3			6	7	2	9	10	11		1	4	8	5	32
		3		5	6	7	2	9	10	11	12	1	4	8*		33
	2			5	6	7		9	10	11	3	1	4	8		34
	2			5	6	7		9	10	11	3	1	4	8		35
		3	4	5	6	7	10	9		11	2	1		8		36
		3	4	5	6	7	10	9		11	2	1		8		37
	2				6	7	8	9		11	3	1	4	10	5	38
	2	12			6	7	8	9*		11	3	1	4	10	5	39
	2		4		6	7	12	9	10*	11	3	1		8	5	40
	2		4	5	6	7	10	9		11	3	1		8		41
	2	6	4	5		7	10	9		11	3	1		8		42
5	37	12	31	26	41	38	26	40	36	42	33	37	10	32	16	
	1				2	3					2			2		
	3	1	4		4	8	4	12	11	12	1			3	4	

1978-79

1	Aug	19	(h)	Tottenham H	D	1-1	O'Neill	41,223
2		22	(a)	Coventry C	D	0-0		28,622
3		26	(a)	QPR	D	0-0		17,971
4	Sep	2	(h)	West Brom A	D	0-0		28,239
5		9	(h)	Arsenal	W	2-1	Robertson (pen), Bowyer	28,124
6		16	(a)	Manchester U	D	1-1	Bowyer	55,039
7		23	(h)	Middlesbrough	D	2-2	Birtles, O'Neill	26,287
8		30	(a)	Aston Villa	W	2-1	Woodcock, Robertson (pen)	36,735
9	Oct	7	(h)	Wolverhampton W	W	3-1	Birtles 2, O'Neill	29,313
10		14	(a)	Bristol C	W	3-1	Birtles, Robertson 2	26,953
11		21	(h)	Ipswich T	W	1-0	O'Neill	28,911
12		28	(a)	Southampton	D	0-0		22,530
13	Nov	4	(h)	Everton	D	0-0		35,415
14		11	(a)	Tottenham H	W	3-1	Anderson, Robertson, Birtles	50,541
15		18	(h)	QPR	D	0-0		28,036
16		25	(a)	Bolton W	W	1-0	Robertson	25,692
17	Dec	9	(a)	Liverpool	L	0-2		51,469
18		16	(h)	Birmingham C	W	1-0	Gemmill	25,224
19		23	(a)	Manchester C	D	0-0		37,012
20		26	(h)	Derby Co	D	1-1	Woodcock	34,256
21	Jan	13	(a)	Arsenal	L	1-2	Robertson	52,158
22	Feb	3	(a)	Middlesbrough	W	3-1	Birtles 2, Robertson (pen)	31,330
23		24	(h)	Bristol C	W	2-0	Needham, Birtles	28,008
24	Mar	3	(a)	Ipswich T	D	1-1	Birtles	27,198
25		10	(a)	Everton	D	1-1	Barrett	37,435
26		14	(h)	Norwich C	W	2-1	Woodcock 2	24,046
27		24	(h)	Coventry C	W	3-0	Woodcock, Birtles, Needham	29,706
28		28	(h)	Chelsea	W	6-0	O'Neill 3, Woodcock 2, Birtles	24,514
29		31	(h)	Bolton W	D	1-1	Francis	29,015
30	Apr	4	(h)	Aston Villa	W	4-0	Evans (og), Woodcock, Francis, O'Neill	27,066
31		7	(a)	Chelsea	W	3-1	Francis, O'Neill, Bowyer	29,213
32		14	(a)	Derby Co	W	2-1	Birtles, O'Neill	30,256
33		16	(h)	Leeds U	D	0-0		37,397
34		18	(h)	Manchester U	D	1-1	Francis	33,074
35		21	(a)	Birmingham C	W	2-0	Birtles, Robertson	22,189
36		28	(h)	Liverpool	D	0-0		41,898
37		30	(a)	Wolverhampton W	L	0-1		23,616
38	May	2	(h)	Southampton	W	1-0	Francis	20,388
39		5	(a)	Norwich C	D	1-1	Woodcock	17,651
40		9	(h)	Manchester C	W	3-1	Birtles, Bowyer, Woodcock	21,104
41		15	(a)	Leeds U	W	2-1	Mills, Hawley (og)	33,544
42		18	(a)	West Brom A	W	1-0	Francis	28,246

FINAL LEAGUE POSITION : 2nd in Division One

Appearances

Sub. Appearances

Goals

Shilton	Anderson	Barrett	McGovern	Needham	Burns	O'Neill	Gemmill	Withe	Woodcock	Robertson	Elliott	Lloyd	Mills	Bowyer	Birtles	O'Hare	Clark	Francis	Gunn	#
1	2	3	4	5	6	7	8	9	10	11										1
1	2	3	4	5	6	7	8		10	11	9									2
1	2	3	4	5	6	7	8		10	11	9									3
1	2	3	4	5	6	7	8		10	11	9									4
1	2	3	4	12	6				10	11		5	7*	8	9					5
1	2	3	4		6	7			10	11		5		8	9					6
1	2	3*	4		6	7			10	11		5		8	9	12				7
1	2		4		6	7	8		10	11		5		3	9					8
1	2		4		6	7	8		10*	11		5		12	9		3			9
1	2		4		6	7	8			11		5			9	10	3			10
1	2		4	5	6	7			10	11				8	9		3			11
1	2		4*	12	6	7			10	11		5		3	9	8				12
1	2				6	7	8		10	11		5		3	9	4				13
1	2		4			7			10	11		5	8	3	9	6				14
1	2		4				8		10	11		5	7	3	9	6				15
1	2		4			7	8		10	11		5*		6	9	12	3			16
1	2	8	4			7				11	9	5		6	10		3			17
1	2		4	5			8		10	11		6		7	9		3			18
1	2		4		6	7	8		10	11		5		12	9*		3			19
1	2		4		6	7	8		10	11		5			9		3			20
1	2		4	5		7	8		10	11		6			9		3			21
1	2		4		6	7	8		10	11		5		3	9					22
1	2		4		6	7*	8		10	11		5			9		3	12		23
1	2		4		6	7	8			11		5			9		3	10		24
1	2		4		6				10	11		5		3	9	8		7		25
1	2		4		6		8		10	11		5			9		3	7		26
1	2	3	4		6	7			10	11		5			9			8		27
1	2		4		6	7			10	11		5		3	9			8		28
1	2		4		6	7			10	11		5		3	9			8		29
1	2		4		6	7	8		10	11		5		3				9		30
1	2		4		6	7	8*			11		5		10		12		9	3	31
1	2			5	6	7			10	11		4			9		3	8		32
1	2		4		6	7				11		5		8	9		3	10		33
1	2	3	4		6	7			10	11		5		8				9		34
1	2		4		6	7			10	11		5			9		3	8		35
1	2		4		6	7			10	11		5			9		3	8		36
1	2		4		6				10	11		5		3	9	7		8		37
1	2		4		6				10	11		5		8	9		3	7		38
1	2		4		6				10	11		5		8	9		3	7		39
1	2		4		6	7*			10	11		5		12	9		3	8		40
1	2		12		6					11		5	7	10	9	4	3*	8		41
1	2		4		6				10	11		5		3	9	7		8		42
42	40	11	36	23	25	28	24	1	36	42	4	36	4	26	35	9	20	19	1	
			3										3	3			1			
		1	1		2		10	1		10	9		1	4	14			6		

31

1979-80

1	Aug	18	(a)	Ipswich T	W	1-0	Woodcock	27,371
2		22	(h)	Stoke C	W	1-0	O'Neill	26,147
3		25	(h)	Coventry C	W	4-1	Woodcock, McGovern 2, Robertson	23,025
4	Sep	1	(a)	West Brom A	W	5-1	Lloyd, Birtles 3, Gray	26,026
5		8	(h)	Leeds U	D	0-0		26,914
6		15	(a)	Norwich C	L	1-3	Woodcock	18,621
7		22	(a)	Bristol C	D	1-1	Mills	22,759
8		29	(h)	Liverpool	W	1-0	Birtles	28,262
9	Oct	6	(h)	Wolverhampton W	W	3-2	Francis, Robertson (pen), Birtles	27,569
10		10	(a)	Stoke C	D	1-1	Birtles	28,514
11		13	(a)	Manchester C	L	0-1		41,683
12		20	(h)	Bolton W	W	5-2	Lloyd, Woodcock, Francis, Robertson (pen), Anderson	24,564
13		27	(a)	Tottenham H	L	0-1		49,038
14	Nov	3	(h)	Ipswich T	W	2-0	Francis 2	24,593
15		10	(a)	Southampton	L	1-4	Birtles	22,072
16		17	(h)	Brighton & HA	L	0-1		25,837
17		24	(a)	Derby Co	L	1-4	Robertson (pen)	27,729
18	Dec	1	(h)	Arsenal	D	1-1	Birtles	27,925
19		8	(a)	Crystal Palace	L	0-1		34,782
20		22	(a)	Manchester U	L	0-3		54,522
21		26	(h)	Aston Villa	W	2-1	Robertson (pen), Bowles	30,979
22		29	(a)	Coventry C	W	3-0	Robertson 2 (1 pen), Bowles	24,737
23	Jan	1	(a)	Everton	L	0-1		34,616
24		12	(h)	West Brom A	W	3-1	Needham, Francis, Anderson	27,724
25		19	(a)	Leeds U	W	2-1	Birtles, Francis	29,816
26	Feb	9	(h)	Bristol C	D	0-0		23,421
27		16	(h)	Middlesbrough	D	2-2	Robertson (pen), O'Neill	28,889
28		19	(a)	Liverpool	L	0-2		45,093
29		23	(h)	Manchester C	W	4-0	Francis 3, Burns	27,244
30	Mar	1	(a)	Bolton W	L	0-1		16,164
31		11	(h)	Tottenham H	W	4-0	Burns 2, Francis 2	25,633
32		22	(h)	Southampton	W	2-0	Robertson (pen), Birtles	27,625
33		29	(a)	Brighton & HA	L	0-1		25,123
34	Apr	2	(h)	Manchester U	W	2-0	Robertson (pen), Birtles	31,417
35		5	(a)	Aston Villa	L	2-3	Birtles, Bowyer	29,156
36		19	(h)	Derby Co	W	1-0	Gray	32,266
37		26	(a)	Middlesbrough	D	0-0		17,021
38		30	(h)	Norwich C	W	2-0	Bond (og), Francis	21,242
39	May	3	(h)	Crystal Palace	W	4-0	Francis 2, Lloyd, Robertson	24,529
40		5	(a)	Arsenal	D	0-0		34,632
41		9	(h)	Everton	W	1-0	Anderson	22,122
42		12	(a)	Wolverhampton W	L	1-3	O'Neill	21,725

FINAL LEAGUE POSITION : 5th in Division One

Appearances

Sub. Appearances

Goals

Shilton	Anderson	Gray	McGovern	Lloyd	Needham	O'Neill	Hartford	Birtles	Woodcock	Robertson	Bowyer	Burns	Mills	O'Hare	Francis	Bowles	George	Gunn	
1	2	3	4	5	6	7	8	9	10	11									1
1	2	3	4	5	6	7	8*	9	10	11	12								2
1	2	3	4	5		7	8	9	10	11		6							3
1	2	3	4	5		7		9	10	11		8	6						4
1	2	3	4	5		7		9	10	11		8	6						5
1	2	3	4	5		7		9	10	11		8	6						6
1	2	3	4	5				9	10	11		6		7	8				7
1	2	3	4	5		7		9	10	11		6			8				8
1	2	3	4	5				9	10	11		6		8	7				9
1	2	3	4	5				9	10	11		6		8	7				10
1	2	3	4	5				9	10	11		6		8	7				11
1	2	3	4	5				9	10	11	12	6		8*	7				12
1	2	3	4	5				9	10	11		6		7	8				13
1	2	3	4	5				9*	10	11		6	12	8	7				14
1	2	3	4	5	12			9	10	11	8	6*			7				15
1	2	3	4	5	6	7		9	10*	11	12				8				16
1	2	3	4	5	6	7		9		11			8		10				17
1	2	3	4	5		7		9		11		6	8		10				18
1	2	3		5		7		9		11	4	6	8		10				19
1	2	3	4	5		7		9		11		6			10	8			20
1	2	3	4	5				9		11	7	6			10	8			21
1	2	3	4	5				9		11	10	6			7	8			22
1	2	3	4	5				9		11	10	6			7	8			23
1	2	3	4	5	6	7		9		11			12		10*	8			24
1	2	3	4	5	6			9		10			7		11	8			25
1	2		4	5		7		9		11		6	8		10		3		26
1	2	3	4	5		7		9		11	12	6			10	8*			27
1	2	3	4	5		7		9		11	8	6			10				28
1	2	3	4	5		7		9		11		6			10	8			29
1		3	4	5		7		9		11		6			10	8	2		30
1	2	3	4	5		10		9		11	12	6			7	8*			31
1	2	3	4	5		7		9		11		6			10	8			32
1	2	3	4	5		7		9		11		6			10	8			33
1	2	3	4	5		7		9		11		6			10	8			34
1	2	3	4	5		7		9		11	12	6			10	8*			35
1	2	3	4	5	6	7		9		11					10	8			36
1	2	3	4	5	6			9		11	8		7		10				37
1	2	3	4	5				9		11		6	7		10	8			38
1	2	3*	4	5		7		9		11		6	12		10	8			39
1	2	3	4	5		7		9		11	8	6			10				40
1	2	3	4	5		7		9*		11	12	6			10	8			41
1	2	3	4	5	12	7		9		11	8	6*			10				42
42	41	41	41	42	8	28	3	42	16	42	12	34	10	7	30	19	2	2	
					2								7	3					
		3	2	2	3	1	3		12	4	11	1	3	1		14	2		

1980-81

1	Aug	16	(a)	Tottenham H	L	0-2		43,272
2		20	(h)	Birmingham C	W	2-1	Birtles, Ponte	26,501
3		23	(a)	Everton	D	0-0		25,981
4		30	(h)	Stoke C	W	5-0	Wallace 2, Birtles 2, Robertson (pen)	21,915
5	Sep	6	(a)	Middlesbrough	D	0-0		17,119
6		13	(h)	Manchester C	W	3-2	Birtles, Bowyer, Wallace	23,184
7		20	(h)	Leicester C	W	5-0	Gray F, Birtles 2, Robertson (pen), Mills	27,145
8		27	(a)	Arsenal	L	0-1		37,584
9	Oct	4	(h)	Manchester U	L	1-2	Wallace	29,801
10		8	(a)	Sunderland	D	2-2	Mills, Bowyer	30,515
11		11	(a)	Brighton & HA	W	1-0	Wallace	17,420
12		18	(h)	West Brom A	W	2-1	Bowyer, Mills	25,096
13		22	(h)	Leeds U	W	2-1	Burns, Wallace	25,033
14		25	(a)	Norwich C	D	1-1	Robertson	17,849
15	Nov	1	(h)	Southampton	W	2-1	Ward, Robertson (pen)	24,669
16		8	(a)	Liverpool	D	0-0		43,143
17		11	(a)	Birmingham C	L	0-2		22,443
18		15	(h)	Tottenham H	L	0-3		25,400
19		22	(h)	Ipswich T	L	1-2	Wallace	24,423
20		29	(a)	Coventry C	D	1-1	Wallace	16,575
21	Dec	6	(h)	Crystal Palace	W	3-0	Gray F (pen), Walsh, Ward	20,223
22		13	(a)	Leeds U	L	0-1		21,882
23		20	(h)	Sunderland	W	3-1	Ponte, Walsh, Francis	23,151
24		26	(a)	Wolverhampton W	W	4-1	Brazier (og), Gray F (pen), Palmer (og), Ponte	31,588
25		27	(h)	Aston Villa	D	2-2	Francis, O'Neill	33,930
26	Jan	10	(a)	Ipswich T	L	0-2		25,701
27		31	(h)	Everton	W	1-0	Burns	25,631
28	Feb	7	(a)	Manchester C	D	1-1	Francis	39,524
29		18	(a)	Stoke C	W	2-1	Doyle (og), Walsh	17,305
30		21	(h)	Arsenal	W	3-1	O'Neill 2, Burns	25,357
31		28	(a)	Leicester C	D	1-1	Walsh	26,608
32	Mar	3	(h)	Middlesbrough	W	1-0	Burns	19,690
33		14	(h)	Brighton & HA	W	4-1	Robertson (pen), Wallace, Mills, Burns	20,688
34		18	(a)	Manchester U	D	1-1	Wallace	38,205
35		21	(a)	West Brom A	L	1-2	Mills	19,269
36		28	(h)	Norwich C	W	2-1	Francis 2	22,353
37	Apr	4	(a)	Southampton	L	0-2		22,712
38		11	(h)	Liverpool	D	0-0		27,363
39		18	(a)	Aston Villa	L	0-2		34,707
40		20	(h)	Wolverhampton W	W	1-0	Francis	19,711
41		25	(a)	Crystal Palace	W	3-1	Gray S, Wallace, Aas	12,138
42	May	2	(h)	Coventry C	D	1-1	Robertson (pen)	21,511

FINAL LEAGUE POSITION : 7th in Division One

Appearances

Sub. Appearances

Goals

34

Shilton	Gunn	Gray F	McGovern	Needham	Burns	Ponte	Bowyer	Birtles	Wallace	Robertson	Anderson	O'Neill	Lloyd	Mills	Ward	Sutton	Walsh	Francis	Gray S	Smelt	Aas	
1	2	3	4	5	6	7	8	9	10	11												1
1		3*	4	5	6	8	12	9	10	11	2	7										2
1		3	4	5	6	7	8	9	10	11	2											3
1		3	4		6		8	9	10	11	2	7	5									4
1		3	4	5	6		8	9	10	11	2	7										5
1		3	4	5	6		8	9	10	11	2	7										6
1		3	4	5	6	8		9	10*	11	2	7		12								7
1		3	4	5	6	8*	12	9		11	2	7		10								8
1		3	4		6	8		9	10	11	2*	7	5	12								9
1	2	3	4		6		8		10	11		7	5	9								10
1	2	3	4		6		8		10	11		7	5	9								11
1	2	3			6	4	8		10	11		7	5	9								12
1	2	3			6	4	8		10	11		7*	5	12	9							13
	2	3	4		6		8		10	11		7	5		9	1						14
1		3			6	4	8		10	11	2	7	5		9							15
1		3	4		6		8		10	11	2	7	5		9							16
1	2	3	4		6		8		10	11		7	5		9							17
1		3			6	4*	8		10	11	2	12	5	7	9							18
1		3	4		6		8		10	11	2		5	7	9							19
1	6	3				4	8		10	11*	2		5	7	9		12					20
1	6	3	4			8*			10		2	12	5	7	9		11					21
1	6	3	4		12				10		2	8	5	7*	9		11					22
1	6	3	4			8			10		2	7	5				11	9				23
1	6	3	4			8			10		2	7	5	12			11	9*				24
1	6	3	4			7			10	11	2	8	5					9				25
1		3	4	5	6		10			11	2	7		8				9				26
1	6	3	4	5		7	8			11	2						10	9				27
1	6	3		5			8			11	2	7					10	9	4			28
1	6	3		5			8			11	2	12		7			10*	9	4			29
1	6	3		5			10			11	2	8		7				9	4			30
1	6	3		5	12		8			11	2	7*					10	9	4			31
1	6	3		5	12		8			11	2	7*					10	9	4			32
1	2	3		5	6	7	8			11				9	12		10		4*			33
1	2	3		5	6	7*	8			11				9	12		10		4			34
	2	3		5	6	12	8			11				7			10*	9	4	1		35
1		3	5*		6	7	8			11	2						10	9	4		12	36
1		3			6		8			11	2			7			10	9	4		5	37
1		3	4	5						11	2			7	8			9	10		6	38
1		3	4		6					11	2			7	8			9	10		5	39
1	6	3	4							11	2			7	8		10	9			5	40
1		3	4	5					8	11	2			7				9	10		6	41
1	2	3	4	5					8	11				7				9	10		6	42
40	26	40	27	17	30	17	19	9	37	38	31	21	18	23	14	1	15	18	14	1	6	
				4	2							3		4	2		1				1	
		3			5	3	3	6	11	6		3		5	2		4	6	1		1	

1981-82

1	Aug	29	(h)	Southampton	W	2-1	Francis 2	25,234
2		31	(a)	Manchester U	D	0-0		51,496
3	Sep	5	(a)	Birmingham C	L	3-4	Wallace 3	19,035
4		12	(h)	West Brom A	D	0-0		22,618
5		19	(a)	Stoke C	W	2-1	Walsh, Mills	15,653
6		23	(h)	Sunderland	W	2-0	Wallace, Proctor	21,133
7		26	(h)	Brighton & HA	W	2-1	Burns, Wallace	19,220
8	Oct	3	(a)	Tottenham H	L	0-3		34,870
9		10	(a)	Middlesbrough	D	1-1	Fashanu	15,043
10		17	(h)	Coventry C	W	2-1	Wallace 2	20,101
11		24	(a)	Manchester C	D	0-0		34,881
12		31	(h)	Leeds U	W	2-1	Ward, Robertson (pen)	25,272
13	Nov	7	(h)	West Ham U	D	0-0		26,327
14		21	(h)	Arsenal	L	1-2	Fashanu	20,912
15		25	(a)	Sunderland	W	3-2	Walsh, Fashanu, Needham	17,419
16		28	(a)	Aston Villa	L	1-3	Walsh	26,847
17	Dec	5	(h)	Liverpool	L	0-2		24,521
18		12	(a)	Swansea C	W	2-1	Young, Robertson (pen)	17,550
19	Jan	9	(h)	Birmingham C	W	2-1	Ward, Wallace	15,906
20		23	(h)	Notts Co	L	0-2		24,521
21		30	(h)	Stoke C	D	0-0		16,219
22	Feb	6	(a)	West Brom A	L	1-2	Ward	15,006
23		13	(a)	Southampton	L	0-2		21,350
24		16	(a)	Wolverhampton W	D	0-0		11,195
25		20	(a)	Brighton & HA	W	1-0	Ward	17,175
26		27	(h)	Middlesbrough	D	1-1	Gray	16,464
27	Mar	9	(a)	Coventry C	W	1-0	Rober	9,720
28		13	(h)	Manchester C	D	1-1	Ward (pen)	20,927
29		17	(h)	Ipswich T	D	1-1	Plummer	16,686
30		20	(a)	Leeds U	D	1-1	Rober	18,036
31		27	(a)	West Ham U	W	1-0	Needham	24,633
32	Apr	3	(h)	Everton	L	0-1		17,323
33		10	(h)	Wolverhampton W	L	0-1		15,691
34		12	(a)	Notts Co	W	2-1	Bowyer, Plummer	19,403
35		17	(a)	Arsenal	L	0-2		21,986
36		20	(a)	Everton	L	1-2	Rober	15,460
37		24	(h)	Aston Villa	D	1-1	Needham	18,213
38	May	1	(a)	Liverpool	L	0-2		24,633
39		5	(h)	Manchester U	L	0-1		17,323
40		8	(h)	Swansea C	L	0-2		15,037
41		12	(h)	Tottenham H	W	2-0	Davenport, Gray	15,189
42		15	(a)	Ipswich T	W	3-1	Davenport 3	19,937

FINAL LEAGUE POSITION : 12th in Division One

Appearances

Sub. Appearances

Goals

Shilton	Anderson	Gray	McGovern	Burns	Aas	Francis	Ward	Fashanu	Proctor	Robertson	Gunn	Mills	Wallace	Walsh	Needham	Rober	Young	Bowyer	Plummer	Kendall	Sutton	Davenport	Hodge	
1	2	3	4	5	6	7	8	9	10	11														1
1	2	3	4	5	6	7	8	9	10	11														2
1	2	3	4	5*	6			9	10	11	12	7	8											3
1	2	3	4	5	6			9	7	11		10*	8	12										4
1	2	3	4	5	6			9	7			10	8	11										5
1	2	3	4		5			9	10	11	6	7	8											6
1	2	3	4	6	5			9	10	11		7	8											7
1	2	3	4	5				9	10	11*	6	7	8	12										8
1	2	3	12	5				9	7	11	6	4	8	10*										9
1	2	7	4*		6			9	10	11	3		8	12	5									10
1	2	7	4		6			9	10	11*	3		8	12	5									11
1	2	7	4		6		8	9	10	11	3				5									12
1	2	7	4		6*			9	10	11	3		8	12	5									13
1	2	7	4		6		8	9	10*	11	3			12	5									14
1	2	4			6*		8	9	10	11	3	12	7		5									15
1	2	3	4				8	9	12	11	6	7		10	5*									16
1	5	3						9	4	11	6	2	8	10			7							17
1	2	4						9	10	11	3		8			6	7	5						18
1	2	3	7				9		10	11	4		8			6*	5	12						19
1		10*	4					9	7	11	2		8			5	12	6	3					20
1	2		4					9	10	11	3		8			7	5	6						21
1	2	3	4				12	9		11	6			8*		7	5	10						22
1	2	12					10	9		11	3	7		4		8*	5	6						23
1	2	4					9			11	3	7	8			6	5	10						24
1	2	4					9			11	3	7				6	5	10	8					25
1	2	3	4				9				6	7	12	11*			5	10	8					26
1	2	11	4				9		10		6		8			7	5	3						27
1	2	11*	4				9	12	8		6		10			7	5	3	7					28
1	2		4				9		8		6		10			11	5	3	11					29
1	2		4					9	10		6		8			7	5	3						30
1	2		4					9	10	11	6		8			7	5	3	12					31
1		6	4				9*		10	11	2		8			7	5	3	12	2				32
1		6						9	10*	11	4		8			7	5	3	8					33
1	2	3						9	10	11	4					7	5	6	8					34
1	2	3*	12					9	10	11	4					7	5	6	8*					35
1	2		12					9	10	11	3				4	7	5	6						36
1	2							9	8	11	3		10		4	7	5	6						37
	2		12						8	11	3		10		4	7	5*	6		1	9			38
1	2								8*	11	3		10	12	4	7	5	6			9			39
1	2								8*	11	3		10	12	4	7	5	6			9			40
1	2	6						9	7	11	4					8	5	3			10			41
1	2	6	8						12	11	4					7	5	3			10	9*		42
41	39	32	26	7	14	2	14	31	35	36	36	13	28	7	17	21	25	23	7	1	1	5	1	
		1	4				1	1	2		1	1	1	8		1		1	2					
	2		1		2	5	3	1	2		1	9	3	2	3	1	1	2				4		

37

1982-83

1	Aug	29	(a)	West Ham U	W	2-1	Walsh, Robertson (pen)	23,796
2	Sep	1	(h)	Manchester U	L	0-3		23,748
3		4	(h)	Brighton & HA	W	4-0	Wallace 2, Robertson (pen), Walsh	13,709
4		7	(a)	Liverpool	L	3-4	Hodge 2, Davenport	27,145
5		11	(a)	Aston Villa	L	1-4	Robertson (pen)	21,224
6		18	(h)	Watford	W	2-0	Walsh, Birtles	11,550
7		25	(a)	Tottenham H	L	1-4	Birtles	30,662
8	Oct	2	(h)	Stoke C	W	1-0	Birtles	17,122
9		9	(a)	West Brom A	L	1-2	Wallace	13,718
10		16	(h)	Birmingham C	D	1-1	Hodge	14,548
11		23	(h)	Arsenal	W	3-0	Proctor, Birtles, Wallace	17,161
12		30	(a)	Luton T	W	2-0	Wallace, Gunn	12,158
13	Nov	6	(h)	Ipswich T	W	2-1	Robertson (pen), Osman (og)	17,461
14		13	(a)	Southampton	D	1-1	Wallace	18,178
15		20	(a)	Sunderland	W	1-0	Wallace	14,716
16		27	(h)	Manchester C	W	3-0	Young, Birtles 2	18,184
17	Dec	4	(a)	Notts Co	L	2-3	Wallace, Young	23,065
18		11	(h)	Swansea C	W	2-1	Walsh, Proctor	14,585
19		18	(a)	Norwich C	W	1-0	Hodge	14,151
20		27	(h)	Coventry C	W	4-2	Young, Robertson (pen), Birtles, Proctor	24,487
21		28	(a)	Everton	L	1-3	Hodge	25,147
22	Jan	1	(h)	Sunderland	D	0-0		20,382
23		3	(a)	Brighton & HA	D	1-1	Young	10,402
24		15	(h)	West Ham U	W	1-0	Wallace	17,031
25		22	(a)	Manchester U	L	0-2		38,615
26	Feb	5	(h)	Aston Villa	L	1-2	Wilson	16,532
27		19	(h)	West Brom A	D	0-0		21,698
28		26	(a)	Birmingham C	D	1-1	Davenport	12,987
29	Mar	5	(a)	Arsenal	D	0-0		21,698
30		12	(h)	Luton T	L	0-1		14,387
31		16	(a)	Stoke C	L	0-1		14,387
32		19	(a)	Ipswich T	L	0-2		17,534
33		26	(h)	Southampton	L	1-2	Hodge	13,461
34	Apr	2	(h)	Everton	W	2-0	Hodge, Bowyer	14,815
35		5	(a)	Coventry C	W	2-1	Wallace, Robertson (pen)	9,720
36		9	(h)	Tottenham H	D	2-2	Davenport, Bowyer	18,265
37		16	(a)	Watford	W	3-1	Bowyer, Hodge, Davenport	17,537
38		23	(h)	Notts Co	W	2-1	Swain, Proctor	25,554
39		30	(a)	Manchester C	W	2-1	Wallace, Davenport	23,563
40	May	2	(h)	Liverpool	W	1-0	Davenport	25,107
41		7	(h)	Norwich C	D	2-2	Walsh, Bowyer	16,308
42		14	(a)	Swansea C	W	3-0	Wallace 2, Anderson	9,226

FINAL LEAGUE POSITION : 5th in Division One

Appearances

Sub. Appearances

Goals

Sutton	Anderson	Bowyer	Proctor	Young	Todd	Hodge	Wallace	Plummer	Walsh	Robertson	Gunn	Birtles	Van Breukelen	Fairclough	Davenport	Gray S	Ward	Swain	Wigley	Wilson	Smalley	#
1	2	3	4*	5	6	7	8	9	10	11	12											1
1	2	3	4	5	6	7	8	9	10	11												2
	2	3	4	5	6	12	8	7	10	11		9*	1									3
	2	3	4		6	7	8		10	11			1	5	9							4
	2	3	12	5	4	7	8		10	11			1	6*	9							5
	2	6	7	5		8	10			11	3	9	1	4								6
	2		7	5		8	10			11	3	9	1	4	6*		12					7
	2		4		6	7	8*		10	11	3	9	1	5			12					8
	2		4	12	6	7	8		10	11	3	9	1	5*								9
		12	4		6	7	8		10*	11	3	9	1	5				2				10
		6	7	4			8		10*	11	3	9	1	5				2	12			11
		6	7	5	4	10	8			11	3	9	1					2				12
		6	7	5	4	10	8			11	3	9	1					2				13
		3	7	5		10	8	6*		11	4	9	1	12				2				14
		3	7	5		10	8	6*		11	4	9	1	12				2				15
		6	7	5	4	10	8			11	3	9	1					2				16
1		6	7*	5	4	10	8	12		11	3	9						2				17
1		3	7	5	6	10	8			11	4	9						2				18
1		3	7	5	6	10	8			11	4	9						2				19
1		6	7	5	4*	10	8	12		11	3	9						2				20
1		6	7	5	4*	10	8	12		11	3	9						2				21
1		6	7	5	4	10	8	12		11	3	9*						2				22
1		6	7	5	4	10	8			11	3				9			2				23
1		6	7	5	4	10	8			11	3	9						2				24
1		6		5		10	8			11	4	7*		12	9	3		2				25
1		6	7	5	4		8			11	3	9						2	10			26
1	4	6	7	5*		10	8			11	3	9						2	12			27
1	2	6	5	4		10	8			11		9*			12			3		7		28
1	2	6	5	4		10	8			11		9*			12			3		7		29
1	2	6	5	4		10	8			11*		9			12			3		7		30
1	2	6	5			10	8			11*	12	4			9			3		7		31
	2	6				10	8			11	4		1	5	9			3*		7	12	32
	2	3			6	10	8*			11	4		1	5	9				12	7		33
	2	6		4		10	8			11			1	5	9			3	12	7*		34
	2	6	5			10	8	12		11	4		1		9			3		7*		35
	2	6	5		7	10	8			11	4		1		9			3				36
	2	6	5		7	10	8			11	4		1		9			3				37
	2	6	7	5			8		10	11	4		1		9			3				38
	2	6	5		7		8		10	11	4		1		9			3				39
	2	6	5		7		8		10	11	4		1		9			3				40
	2	6	5		7		8		10	11	4		1		9			3				41
	2	6	5		7		8		10	11	4		1		9*			3	12			42
17	25	39	25	34	23	38	41	3	32	33	32	25	25	12	15	2		32		9		
		1	2	1					5	1	1			3	3		2		4	1	1	
	1	4	4	4		8	13		5	6	1	7			6			1		1		

39

1983-84

1	Aug	27	(h)	Southampton	L	0-1		14,626
2		29	(a)	Manchester U	W	2-1	Anderson, Davenport	43,005
3	Sep	3	(a)	Liverpool	L	0-1		31,376
4		7	(h)	Aston Villa	D	2-2	Davenport, Birtles	16,363
5		10	(h)	QPR	W	3-2	Hodge, Davenport, Hazell (og)	14,607
6		17	(a)	Norwich C	W	3-2	Walsh 3	15,017
7		24	(h)	Luton T	W	1-0	Wallace	16,296
8	Oct	2	(a)	Tottenham H	L	1-2	Walsh	30,596
9		16	(h)	Notts Co	W	3-1	Wallace, Bowyer, Davenport	26,658
10		22	(a)	Arsenal	L	1-4	Davenport (pen)	22,870
11		29	(h)	Sunderland	D	1-1	Thijssen	13,968
12	Nov	5	(h)	Wolverhampton W	W	5-0	Birtles, Davenport (pen), Walsh, Hodge 2	13,855
13		12	(a)	Everton	L	0-1		17,546
14		19	(h)	Ipswich T	W	2-1	Birtles, Swain	14,979
15		26	(a)	Stoke C	D	1-1	Walsh (pen)	11,655
16	Dec	4	(h)	Leicester C	W	3-2	Walsh, Bowyer, Thijssen	23,248
17		10	(a)	Watford	L	2-3	Birtles 2	14,047
18		17	(h)	West Ham U	W	3-0	Hodge, Birtles, Walsh (pen)	14,544
19		26	(a)	Birmingham C	W	2-1	Birtles, Hodge	14,482
20		28	(h)	Coventry C	W	3-0	Davenport, Birtles 2	22,169
21		31	(h)	Liverpool	L	0-1		29,692
22	Jan	2	(a)	Luton T	W	3-2	Birtles, Hodge, Davenport	12,126
23		21	(h)	Norwich C	W	3-0	Thijssen, Hodge, Anderson	13,993
24		23	(a)	Southampton	W	1-0	Birtles	17,425
25	Feb	4	(h)	Tottenham H	D	2-2	Hodge, Walsh (pen)	21,428
26		8	(a)	West Brom A	W	5-0	Walsh (pen), McNaught (og), Bowyer, Birtles, Anderson	11,020
27	·	11	(a)	QPR	W	1-0	Birtles	16,692
28		18	(a)	Sunderland	D	1-1	Anderson	15,958
29		25	(h)	Arsenal	L	0-1		20,045
30	Mar	3	(a)	Wolverhampton W	L	0-1		10,476
31		13	(h)	Everton	W	1-0	Hodge	13,647
32		17	(a)	Aston Villa	L	0-1		16,270
33		31	(a)	Notts Co	D	0-0		18,357
34	Apr	7	(h)	West Brom A	W	3-1	Walsh (pen), Anderson, Bowyer	15,245
35		14	(a)	Ipswich T	D	2-2	Wigley, Davenport	15,429
36		17	(a)	Coventry C	L	1-2	Walsh	9,819
37		21	(h)	Birmingham C	W	5-1	Davenport 2, Walsh, Wallace, Bowyer	15,323
38		28	(h)·	Stoke C	D	0-0		13,625
39	May	5	(a)	Leicester C	L	1-2	Davenport	16,600
40		7	(h)	Watford	W	5-1	Atkinson (og), Hodge, Davenport 2, Bowyer	13,732
41		12	(a)	West Ham U	W	2-1	Birtles, Davenport	18,468
42		16	(h)	Manchester U	W	2-0	Birtles, Anderson	23,651

FINAL LEAGUE POSITION : 3rd in Division One

Appearances

Sub. Appearances

Goals

Van Breukelen	Anderson	Swain	Todd	Hart	Bowyer	Walsh	Wallace	Birtles	Hodge	Davenport	Wigley	Fairclough	Smalley	Thijssen	Sutton	Gunn	Walker	Mills	Riley	No.
1	2	3	4	5	6	7*	8	9	10	11	12									1
1	2	3	4	5	6	7	8	9	10	11										2
1	2	3	4	5	6	7	8	9	10	11										3
1	2	3	4	5	6	7	8	9	10	11										4
1	2	3	4	5	6	7*	8	9	10	11	12									5
1	2	3	4		6	7*	8		10	9	11	5	12							6
1	2	3	4	5	6	7	8	9	10		11									7
1	2	3	4	5	6	11	8	9	10		7									8
1	2	3	4	5	6		8		11	9	7			10						9
1	2	3	4	5	6		8		11	9	7			10						10
	2	3	4	5	6		8		11	9	7			10	1					11
	2	3	4		6	12		9	11	8	7	5		10*	1					12
	2	3	4		6	12		9	11	8	7	5		10*	1					13
	2	3		5	6	12		9	11	8	7	4		10*	1					14
	2	3		5	6	11		9	7	10		4		8	1					15
	2	3		5	6	11		9		10	7	4		8	1					16
1	2	3		5	6	11		9	8	10	7	4								17
1	2	3		5*	6	11	12	9	10	8	7	4								18
1	2	3			6	11		9	8	10	7	5				4				19
1	2	3			6	11	12	9	8	10	78	5				4				20
1	2	3		5	6	11	12	9	8	10	7*	4								21
1	2	3		5	6	11	12	9	8	10*	7	4								22
1	2	3		5	6	11	8	9*	10		12	4		7						23
1	2	3		5	6	11	8	9*	10		12	4		7						24
1	2	3		5	6	11	8	9*	10	12		4		7						25
1	2	3		5	6	11	8	9	10		12	4		7*						26
1	2	3		5	6	11	8	9	10			4		7						27
1	2	3		5	6	11	8	9	10		12	4		7*						28
1	2	3		5	6	11	8	9	10		12	4		7*						29
1	2	3		5	6	11	8*	9	10		12	4		7						30
1		3		5	6	11*	12	9	10	8	7	4						2		31
1		3		5	6	11		9	10	8	7	4						2		32
1	2	3		5	6	11	7	9*	10	8		4						12		33
1	2	3		5	6	11			10	9	7	4					8*	12		34
1	2	3		5	6	11			10	9	7					4	8			35
1	2	3		5	6	11			10	9	7	4					8			36
1	2			5	6	11	8			9	7	4		10*		3		12		37
1	2	3		5	6	11		12	8	9	7	4						10*		38
1	2	3		5	6			9	10	8	7	4						11		39
1	2	3		5	6	11		9*	8	10	7	4						12		40
1	2	3		5	6	11		9	8	10	7	4								41
1	2	3			6	11	8	9		10	7	5			4					42
36	40	41	13	36	42	35	22	33	39	32	27	31		17	6	4	3	5		
						3	5	1		1	8		1			1	2	1		
	6	1			6	13	3	15	10	15	1			3						

41

1984-85

1	Aug	25	(a)	Sheffield W	L	1-3	Davenport	31,925
2		29	(h)	Arsenal	W	2-0	Davenport, Metgod	17,972
3	Sep	1	(h)	Sunderland	W	3-1	Davenport 3	15,760
4		5	(a)	Aston Villa	W	5-0	Bowyer, Christie 3, Hodge	17,730
5		8	(a)	QPR	L	0-3		13,507
6		16	(h)	Luton T	W	3-1	Davenport, Hodge 2	18,605
7		22	(a)	West Ham U	D	0-0		17,434
8		29	(h)	Norwich C	W	3-1	Christie, Hodge, Watson (og)	15,166
9	Oct	6	(h)	Stoke C	D	1-1	Davenport (pen)	14,129
10		13	(a)	West Brom A	L	1-4	Bowyer	13,056
11		20	(a)	Newcastle U	D	1-1	Hodge	28,252
12		28	(h)	Liverpool	L	0-2		19,838
13	Nov	3	(a)	Southampton	L	0-1		17,818
14		10	(h)	Tottenham H	L	1-2	Davenport	21,306
15		17	(a)	Coventry C	W	3-1	Adams (og), Riley, Walsh	9,894
16		25	(h)	Leicester C	W	2-1	Davenport 2 (1 pen)	21,463
17	Dec	1	(a)	Watford	L	0-2		17,758
18		8	(h)	Manchester U	W	3-2	Hodge, Metgod, Mills	25,902
19		15	(a)	Everton	L	0-5		22,487
20		23	(a)	Sunderland	W	2-0	Christie, Wigley	21,086
21		26	(h)	Ipswich T	W	2-0	Hodge, Metgod	17,123
22		29	(h)	Aston Villa	W	3-2	Davenport 2 (1 pen), Metgod	17,676
23	Jan	1	(a)	Chelsea	L	0-1		21,552
24	Feb	2	(a)	Norwich C	W	1-0	Davenport	14,669
25		9	(h)	QPR	W	2-0	Hodge, Metgod	12,001
26		23	(h)	Southampton	W	2-0	Davenport (pen), Hodge	14,752
27	Mar	2	(a)	Liverpool	L	0-1		35,696
28		9	(h)	Newcastle U	D	0-0		17,425
29		16	(h)	West Brom A	L	1-2	Davenport	12,663
30		20	(h)	Sheffield W	D	0-0		17,648
31		23	(a)	Stoke C	W	4-1	Davenport, Hart, Hodge, Riley	7,453
32		30	(h)	West Ham U	L	1-2	Hodge	13,560
33	Apr	6	(a)	Ipswich T	L	0-1		16,296
34		10	(h)	Chelsea	W	2-0	Birtles, Metgod	14,666
35		13	(a)	Arsenal	D	1-1	Mills	24,152
36		20	(h)	Coventry C	W	2-0	Hibbit (og), Mills	12,990
37		24	(a)	Luton T	W	2-1	Hodge, Mills	10,156
38		27	(a)	Leicester C	L	0-1		13,886
39	May	4	(h)	Watford	D	1-1	Clough	12,649
40		6	(a)	Manchester U	L	0-2		43,334
41		11	(h)	Everton	W	1-0	Birtles	18,784
42		17	(a)	Tottenham H	L	0-1		20,075

FINAL LEAGUE POSITION : 9th in Division One

Appearances

Sub. Appearances

Goals

Appearances / line-up grid (shirt numbers per match; `*` = substitute)

Sutton	Swain	Bowyer	Fairclough	Hart	Metgod	Wigley	Hodge	Christie	Davenport	Walsh	Mills	Gunn	Smalley	McInally	Raynor	Riley	Segers	Davidson	Clough	Birtles	Campbell	Fleming	Walker	#
1	2	3	4	5	6	7	8	9	10	11*	12													1
1	3	6	4	5	8	7	11	9	10			2												2
1	3	6	4	5	8	7	11	9	10			2												3
1	3	6	4	5	8	7	11	9	10			2												4
1	3	6	4	5	8	7	11	9*	10		12	2												5
1	3	6	4	5	8	7	11	9*	10		12	2												6
1	3	6	4		8	7	9		10	11		2	5											7
1	3	6	5		8	7*	11	9	10		12	4		2										8
1	3	6	4	5	8	7	11	9*	10	12		2												9
1	3	6	4	5	8	7	11	9*	10		12	2												10
1	3	6	4	5	8	7	11	9	10			2												11
1	3	6	5		4		8	9	10	11	7	2												12
1	3	6	5		4	7	8			11		2			9	10									13
1	3	6	5		4	7	8		10	11		2			9										14
	3	6	5		4	7	8		10	11		2			9*	12	1							15
	3	6	5		4	7	8		10	11		2			9		1							16
	3	10	4	5	8		11	9			7	6					1	2						17
	3	6	4	5	8		11	10			7				9		1	2						18
	3	6	4	5	8	7	11	10			12	2*					1			9				19
	3	6	4	5	8	7	11	9	10					2			1							20
	3	6	4	5	8	7	11		10					2			1			9				21
	3	6		5	8	7	11	9	10		4			2			1							22
			5		8	7	11	9	10	6	4			2			1	3						23
	3		4	5	8	7	11		10	6				2			1		9					24
	3		4	5	8	7	11		10	6				2			1			9				25
	3	6	4	5	8	7	11		10					2			1			9				26
	3	6	4	5	8	7	11		10					2		12	1		9*					27
	3	6	4	5	8	7	11		10					2			1		9					28
	3	6		5	8	7	11		10		4			2		12	1		9*					29
	3	6	4	5		7	8		10	11				2	9		1							30
	3	6	4*	5	8	7	11		10		12			2	9		1							31
	3	6	4	5	8	7	11		10					2	9		1				12			32
	3	6	4	5	8	7	11		10		12			2			1		9*					33
	3	6	4	5	8	7			10	11				2			1		9*					34
		6	4	5	8	7			10	11				2			1		9		2			35
		6	4	5	8	7		9	10*	11				2			1		12		2			36
	3*	6	4	5	8		11	10			7	4		2			1		9	12				37
	3	6*		5	8		11	12			7	4		2			1		9	10				38
	3	6		5	8*	12	11				7			2			1		9	10				39
	3	6		5		7	11				8			2			1		9	10		4		40
	3	6		5	8		11				7			2			1		9	10		4		41
	3	6		5	8		11		10		7			2			1		9			4		42
14	39	39	35	34	40	34	42	14	35	10	18	17	1	24	3	7	28	3	8	12	2	3		
				1							3	7				3				1	1	1			
	2		1	6	1	12	5	16			1	4			2				1	2				

43

1985-86

1	Aug	17	(a)	Luton T	D	1-1	Webb	11,318
2		21	(h)	Sheffield W	L	0-1		18,367
3		24	(h)	Southampton	W	2-1	Metgod, Wright (og)	12,643
4		27	(a)	QPR	L	1-2	Webb	10,748
5		31	(h)	Manchester U	L	1-3	Davenport	26,274
6	Sep	3	(a)	Liverpool	L	0-2		27,135
7		8	(a)	Leicester C	W	3-0	Webb, Davenport, Rice	14,247
8		14	(h)	Tottenham H	L	0-1		17,554
9		21	(h)	Watford	W	3-2	Clough, Campbell, Davenport	12,921
10		28	(a)	West Ham U	L	2-4	Metgod, Clough	14,540
11	Oct	5	(h)	Ipswich T	W	3-1	Pearce, Bowyer 2	12,120
12		12	(a)	Aston Villa	W	2-1	Ormsby (og), Clough	15,315
13		19	(a)	Newcastle U	W	3-0	Rice, Davenport 2	23,151
14		26	(h)	Arsenal	W	3-2	Davenport 3 (1 pen)	17,756
15	Nov	3	(h)	West Brom A	W	2-1	Webb, Davenport (pen)	19,610
16		9	(a)	Chelsea	L	2-4	Clough 2	17,743
17		16	(h)	Manchester C	L	0-2		15,140
18		23	(a)	Everton	D	1-1	Clough	27,860
19	Dec	1	(h)	Oxford U	D	1-1	Davenport (pen)	15,317
20		7	(a)	Sheffield W	L	1-2	Webb	22,495
21		14	(h)	Luton T	W	2-0	Clough, Webb	12,078
22		20	(a)	Southampton	L	1-3	Carr	12,500
23		26	(a)	Birmingham C	W	1-0	Webb	10,378
24		28	(h)	Liverpool	D	1-1	Webb	27,141
25	Jan	1	(h)	Coventry C	W	5-2	Webb 3, Metgod, Davenport	13,860
26		11	(a)	Tottenham H	W	3-0	Davenport 2, Walsh	19,043
27		18	(a)	Manchester U	W	3-2	Walsh 2, Clough	46,717
28	Feb	1	(h)	QPR	W	4-0	Walsh 2, Carr, Webb	11,538
29		8	(h)	Newcastle U	L	1-2	Walsh	15,388
30	Mar	8	(a)	Ipswich T	L	0-1		12,658
31		15	(h)	Aston Villa	D	1-1	Clough (pen)	12,933
32		22	(h)	Leicester C	W	4-3	Bowyer, Carr, Clough 2	14,484
33		29	(a)	Coventry C	D	0-0		9,500
34		31	(h)	Birmingham C	W	3-0	Clough (pen), Metgod, Webb	13,134
35	Apr	2	(h)	West Ham U	W	2-1	Metgod, Rice	17,498
36		5	(a)	West Brom A	D	1-1	Metgod	7,901
37		8	(a)	Arsenal	D	1-1	Campbell	15,098
38		12	(h)	Chelsea	D	0-0		18,055
39		19	(a)	Manchester C	W	2-1	Webb, Campbell	19,715
40		21	(a)	Watford	D	1-1	Clough	11,510
41		26	(h)	Everton	D	0-0		30,171
42	May	3	(a)	Oxford U	W	2-1	Clough 2	11,845

FINAL LEAGUE POSITION : 8th in Division One

Appearances

Sub. Appearances

Goals

44

Segers	McInally	Pearce	Butterworth	Walker	Hodge	Mills	Webb	Birtles	Davenport	Robertson	Wigley	Metgod	Clough	Bowyer	Rice	Campbell	Walsh	Sutton	Carr	Williams	Fleming	
1	2	3	4	5	6	7	8	9	10	11												1
1	2	3	4	5	6		8	9	10	11	7											2
1	2	3	4	5			6	9	10	11	7	8										3
1	2	3	4	5		12	6		10	11*	7	8	9									4
1	2*	3	4	5			6		10	11	7	8	9	12								5
1		3	2	4			8	9*	10		7	5	12	6	11							6
1		3	2	4			8*		10		7	5	12	6	11							7
1		3	4	2			8		10		7	5	9	6	11							8
1		3	4	2			8		10		7	5	9	6*	11	12						9
1*		3	4	2		7	11		10			5	9	6			8	12				10
	2	3	4	5			12		10	11		7	9	6		8*		1				11
		3	4			2	6	5	10			8	9		11			1	7			12
		3	4			2	6	5	10			8	9		11			1	7			13
		3	4	12		2	6	5	10			8*	9		11			1	7			14
		3	4			2	6	5	10			8	9		11			1	7			15
		3	4	12		2	6	5	10			8	9		11*			1	7			16
		3	4	12		2	6	5*	10			8	9		11			1	7			17
	2	3	5	4		7	6		10			8	9				11	1				18
	2	3		4		7	6	5	10			8	9				11	1				19
	2	3	5	4			8	5	10				9	6			11	1	7			20
	2	3	5	4			10			11		8*	9	6			12	1	7			21
	2			4			10	3*		11		12	9	6			8	1	7			22
	2*			4			8	5	10	11		7	9	6			12	1		3		23
				4		2	8	5	10	11		7	9	6				1		3		24
		3		4		2	8	5	10	11		7	9	6				1		3		25
				4			8	5	10	12		7	9*	6			11	1		3		26
				4			8		10			5	9	6			11	1	7	3	2	27
				4			8		10			5	9	6	12		11	1	7*	3	2	28
				4			8		10			5	9	6	12		11	1	7*	3	2	29
				4			8		10			5	9	6	11*	12		1	7	3	2	30
1				4		7	10	5				12	9	6	8		11*			3	2	31
				4			10					5	9	6	11	8		1	7	3	2	32
				4			10					5	9	6	11	8		1	7	3	2	33
		3		4			8	10*				5	9	6	11	7	12	1			2	34
		3		4			8					5	9	6	11	10		1	7		2	35
		3	5	4								10	9		11	8	6	1	7		2	36
		3		4			10					5	9	6	8	11		1	7		2	37
		3		4			8					5	9	6	10	11		1	7		2	38
		3	12	4			8					5	9	6*	10	11		1	7		2	39
		3		4			8					5	9		11	10	6	1	7		2	40
		3		4			8					5	9		11	10	6	1	7		2	41
		3		4			8					5	9		11	10	6	1	7		2	42
11	12	30	22	36	2	13	38	24	27	10	8	37	37	25	19	14	16	31	23	11	16	
		1	3	1		1			1			2	2	1		4	4					
		1					14		13			6	15	3	3	3	6		3			

45

1986-87

1	Aug	23	(a)	Everton	L	0-2		35,198
2		27	(h)	Charlton Ath	W	4-0	Webb 2, Birtles, Clough	12,970
3		30	(h)	Watford	D	1-1	Bowyer	14,723
4	Sep	2	(a)	West Ham U	W	2-1	Clough, Webb	21,305
5		6	(a)	Southampton	W	3-1	Webb 2, Birtles	14,604
6		13	(h)	Aston Villa	W	6-0	Carr, Birtles 2, Clough, Webb 2	17,045
7		20	(a)	Chelsea	W	6-2	Webb 3, Birtles 3 (1 pen)	20,171
8		27	(h)	Arsenal	W	1-0	Clough	25,371
9	Oct	4	(h)	Manchester U	D	1-1	Birtles	34,828
10		11	(a)	Leicester C	L	1-3	Birtles	18,402
11		18	(h)	QPR	W	1-0	Clough	17,199
12		25	(a)	Oxford U	L	1-2	Pearce (pen)	10,219
13	Nov	1	(h)	Sheffield W	W	3-2	Webb, Pearce (pen), Birtles	23,303
14		8	(a)	Coventry C	L	0-1		16,089
15		15	(a)	Luton T	L	2-4	Bowyer, Birtles	11,097
16		22	(h)	Wimbledon	W	3-2	Clough (pen), Thorn (og), Metgod	15,481
17		29	(a)	Tottenham H	W	3-2	Pearce (pen), Fairclough, Webb	30,042
18	Dec	6	(h)	Manchester C	W	2-0	Birtles, Carr	19,129
19		13	(a)	Newcastle U	L	2-3	Starbuck, Carr	26,191
20		20	(h)	Southampton	D	0-0		15,394
21		26	(a)	Norwich C	L	1-2	Pearce	22,131
22		28	(h)	Luton T	D	2-2	Clough, Bowyer	20,273
23	Jan	1	(h)	Liverpool	D	1-1	Starbuck	32,854
24		3	(a)	Aston Villa	D	0-0		19,159
25		25	(h)	Everton	W	1-0	Webb	17,009
26		31	(a)	Charlton Ath	W	1-0	Clough	5,050
27	Feb	7	(a)	Watford	D	1-1	Birtles	15,173
28		14	(h)	West Ham U	D	1-1	Birtles (pen)	19,373
29		28	(h)	Chelsea	L	0-1		18,317
30	Mar	7	(h)	Oxford U	W	2-0	Clough 2	12,298
31		14	(a)	QPR	L	1-3	Metgod	11,896
32		17	(a)	Arsenal	D	0-0		18,352
33		22	(h)	Leicester C	W	2-1	Carr, Clough	18,679
34		28	(a)	Manchester U	L	0-2		39,182
35	Apr	4	(h)	Coventry C	D	0-0		13,507
36		14	(a)	Sheffield W	W	3-2	Clough 2, Rice	18,597
37		18	(a)	Liverpool	L	0-3		37,359
38		20	(h)	Norwich C	D	1-1	Clough	14,446
39		25	(a)	Wimbledon	L	1-2	Pearce (pen)	5,012
40	May	2	(h)	Tottenham H	W	2-0	Webb, Metgod	19,837
41		4	(a)	Manchester C	L	0-1		21,405
42		9	(h)	Newcastle U	W	2-1	Foster, Pearce (pen)	17,788

FINAL LEAGUE POSITION : 8th in Division One

Appearances

Sub. Appearances

Goals

Sutton	Fleming	Pearce	Walker	Metgod	Bowyer	Carr	Webb	Clough	Birtles	Campbell	Mills	Fairclough	Segers	Butterworth	Williams	Starbuck	Foster	Wilkinson	Rice	Osvold	Riley	#
1	2	3	4	5	6	7	8	9	10	11												1
1	2	3	4	5	6	7	8	9*	10	11	12											2
1	2	3	4	5	6	7	8	9	10	11												3
1	2	3	4	5	6	7	8	9	10	11												4
1	2	3	4	5	6	7	8	9	10	11												5
1	2	3	4	5	6*	7	8	9	10	11	12											6
1	2	3	4	5	6	7	8	9	10	11*	12											7
1	2	3		5	6	7	8	9	10	11		4										8
1	2	3	4	5	6	7	8	9	10	11												9
1*	2	3	4	5	6	7	8	9	10	11	12											10
	2	3	4	5	6	7		9	10	8	11		1									11
	2	3	4	5	6	7	8	9	10	11*		12	1									12
		3	4	5	6	7	8	9	10		11		1	2								13
		3	4	5	6	7	8	9	10		11		1	2								14
		3	4	5	6	7	8	9	10		11		1	2								15
			4	5	6	7	8	9	10		11		1	2	3							16
	2	3	4	8		7	6	9	10		11	5	1									17
	2	3	4	8		7	6	9	10		11	5	1									18
	2	3	4	8	6	7	11	9				5	1				10					19
	2	3	4	8		7	6	9	10		11	5	1									20
	2	3	4	8	6	7	11	9		10		5	1									21
	2	3	4		6	7	8	9		10	11	5	1									22
	2	3	4		6	7	8	9			11	5	1				10					23
	2	3	4		6	7	8	9			11	5	1				10					24
1	2	3	4	10	6	7	8	9			11	5										25
1	2	3	4	10	6	7	8	9			11	5										26
1	2	3	4		6	7	8	9	10		11	5										27
1	2		4		6	7	8	9	10		11	5			3							28
1	2		4	8	6	7		9	10		11	5			3							29
1	2	3	4	12	6	7	8*	9	10		11	5										30
1	2	3	4	8	6	7		9	10	11*		5					12					31
1		3	2	4	6	7	8*	9	10		11	5					12					32
1	2	3	4	8	6	7		9	10	11		5										33
1	2	3	4	8	6		9	10*		11		5					12	7				34
1	2	3	4	8	6		9	10			7	5							11			35
1	2	3	4	6		7		9				5					10	11				36
1	2	3	4	8	6	7		9		12		5					10*	11				37
1	2	3	4	8	6	7*		9		11	12	5					10					38
1	2	3	4	8			9	7	6		12	5					10*	11				39
1		3	2	6		8	9	7		4		5					10	11				40
1		3	2	6		8	9	7		4		5					10*	11	12			41
1		3	2	6	3		9	7		4		5					10	11				42
28	34	39	41	36	34	36	32	42	22	14	27	24	14	4	3	3	7	8	3	4		
			1									5	2				2	2		1		
	6			3		3	4	14	14	14		1					2	1	1			

47

1987-88

1	Aug	15	(a)	Charlton Ath	W	2-1	Glover, Clough	6,021
2		19	(h)	Watford	W	1-0	Pearce (pen)	14,527
3		22	(h)	Everton	D	0-0		20,445
4		29	(a)	Newcastle U	W	1-0	Clough	20,111
5	Sep	2	(h)	Southampton	D	3-3	Webb, Pearce, Clough	14,173
6		5	(a)	Chelsea	L	3-4	Foster, Clough, Wilkinson	18,414
7		12	(h)	Arsenal	L	0-1		18,490
8		19	(a)	Coventry C	W	3-0	Wilson, Carr, Pearce (pen)	17,519
9		26	(a)	Norwich C	W	2-0	Webb 2	13,755
10	Oct	10	(a)	Derby Co	W	1-0	Wilkinson	22,395
11		17	(h)	Sheffield W	W	3-0	Clough, Carr, Wilkinson	17,685
12		24	(h)	Tottenham H	W	3-0	Carr, Webb, Clough	23,543
13		31	(a)	Manchester U	D	2-2	Wilkinson, Pearce	44,669
14	Nov	14	(h)	Portsmouth	W	5-0	Wilson, Wilkinson, Webb, Rice, Clough (pen)	15,851
15		21	(a)	West Ham U	L	2-3	Webb, Clough	17,216
16	Dec	5	(a)	Wimbledon	D	1-1	Clough	5,170
17		13	(h)	QPR	W	4-0	Gaynor, Clough 3 (1 pen)	18,130
18		19	(a)	Oxford U	W	2-0	Rice, Plummer	7,891
19		26	(a)	Arsenal	W	2-0	Wilson , Pearce (pen)	31,211
20		28	(h)	Coventry C	W	4-1	Gaynor 2, Borrows (og), Wilson	31,060
21	Jan	1	(h)	Newcastle U	L	0-2		28,583
22		3	(a)	Everton	L	0-1		21,680
23		16	(h)	Charlton Ath	D	2-2	Plummer, Webb	15,363
24		23	(a)	Watford	D	0-0		13,158
25	Feb	6	(h)	Chelsea	W	3-2	Foster, Crosby, Clough (pen)	18,203
26		13	(a)	Southampton	D	1-1	Clough	13,315
27	Mar	5	(a)	Sheffield W	W	1-0	Webb	19,509
28		16	(a)	QPR	L	1-2	Maddix (og)	8,316
29		19	(h)	Manchester U	D	0-0		27,598
30		26	(a)	Tottenham H	D	1-1	Clough	25,306
31		30	(h)	Derby Co	W	2-1	Clough 2	25,017
32	Apr	2	(h)	Liverpool	W	2-1	Hansen (og), Webb	29,188
33		4	(a)	Portsmouth	W	1-0	Wilson	17,528
34		13	(a)	Liverpool	L	0-5		39,535
35		20	(h)	West Ham U	D	0-0		15,775
36		30	(h)	Wimbledon	D	0-0		14,341
37	May	4	(h)	Norwich C	W	2-0	Webb, Glover	11,610
38		7	(h)	Oxford U	W	5-3	Webb 2, Carr, Clough 2	12,762
39		13	(a)	Luton T	D	1-1	Glover	9,018
40		15	(h)	Luton T	D	1-1	Webb	13,106

FINAL LEAGUE POSITION : 3rd in Division One   Appearances

Sub. Appearances

Goals

48

Sutton	Fleming	Pearce	Walker	Foster	Campbell	Carr	Webb	Clough	Wilkinson	Glover	Segers	Wilson	Chettle	Starbuck	Rice	Osvold	Gaynor	Plummer	Crosby	Wassall	Williams	Parker	
1	2	3	4	5	6	7	8	9	10	11													1
1	2	3	4	5	6	7	8	9	10	11													2
	2	3	4	5	6	7	8	9	10	11	1												3
	2	3	4	5	6	7	8	9	10	11	1												4
	2*	3	4	5	6	7	8	9	10	11	1	12											5
	2	3	4	5	6*	7	8	9	10	11†	1	12	14										6
	2	3	4	5	6*	7	8	9	10†	11	1	12		14									7
1	2*	3	4	5	12	7	8	9	10			6			11								8
1		3	4	5		7	8	9	10	12		6	2		11*								9
1		3	4	5		7	8	9	10			6	2		11								10
1		3	4	5		7	8	9	10			6*	2		11	12							11
1		3	4	5		7	8	9	10			6*	2		11	12							12
1		3	4	5		7	8	9	10			6	2		11								13
1		3	4	5		7	8	9	10	14		6*	2	12	11†								14
1		3	4	5		7*	8	9	10†			6	2	12	11		14						15
1		3	4	5			8	9				6*	2		11		10		7				16
1	2	3	4	5			8	9				6*		12	11		10		7				17
1		3	4	5			8	9				6	2	12	11		10		7*				18
1		3	4	5			8	9*				6	2	12	11		10		7				19
1	14	3	4	5			8			9		6	2†	12	11		10		7*				20
1	14	3	4	5			8			9†		6	2	12	11		10*		7				21
1	12	3	4	5		7*	8					6	2	9	11		10						22
1		3	4	5			8		12	9*		6	2		11		10†		7		14		23
1		3	4	5			8		10	9		6	2		11				7				24
1	2	3	4	5*			8	9				6	12	14	11†		10		7				25
1	2	3	4				8	9	10			6			11				7	5			26
1	2	3	4	5			8	9	10			6			11			12	7*				27
1		3	4	5			8	9	10			6	2		11			7					28
1		3	4	5			8	9	10			6	2		11			7					29
1	2		4	5			8	9	10			6	3		11			7					30
1		3	4	5			8	9	10			6	2		11			7					31
1		3	4	5			8	9	10			6	2		11			7					32
1		3		5			8	9	10	11		6	2					7			4		33
1		3	4*	5			8	9	10			6	2		11			7			12		34
1	2	3		5		10	8	9				6	4		11			7					35
1	2			5		7	8		12			6	4		11	9*			3		10		36
1	2			5		7	8	9*	12	10		6†	4		11				3		14		37
1	2			5		7	8	9	10			6	4		11				3				38
1	2		4	12		7	8	9	10			6	5		11				3*				39
1	2		4	5		7*	8	9	10			6	3		11				12				40
35	19	34	35	38	7	22	40	34	27	17	5	33	28	1	30	1	10	8	12	2	4	1	
	3		1	1						2	3	3	2	9	2	2			2	1	1		
		5	2		4	13	19	5	3			5			2				3	2	1		

1988-89

1	Aug	27	(a)	Norwich C	L	1-2	Chettle	13,488
2	Sep	3	(h)	Sheffield W	D	1-1	Worthington (og)	18,963
3		10	(a)	Everton	D	1-1	Webb	34,003
4		17	(h)	Derby Co	D	1-1	Foster	24,818
5		24	(a)	Aston Villa	D	1-1	Carr	23,029
6	Oct	1	(h)	Luton T	D	0-0		15,340
7		8	(a)	QPR	W	2-1	Clough (pen), Foster	11,205
8		22	(a)	Millwall	D	2-2	Hodge 2	16,874
9		26	(h)	Liverpool	W	2-1	Rice, Webb	29,755
10		29	(a)	Newcastle U	W	1-0	Chapman	24,765
11	Nov	6	(h)	Arsenal	L	1-4	Clough	19,038
12		12	(a)	West Ham U	D	3-3	Clough 2, Hodge	21,682
13		19	(h)	Coventry C	D	0-0		17,250
14		26	(a)	Charlton Ath	W	1-0	Pearce	6,411
15	Dec	3	(h)	Middlesbrough	D	2-2	Chapman 2	17,742
16		10	(a)	Southampton	D	1-1	Clough	15,259
17		18	(h)	Wimbledon	L	0-1		16,427
18		26	(a)	Manchester U	L	0-2		39,582
19		31	(a)	Sheffield W	W	3-0	Gaynor, Webb, Hodge	20,407
20	Jan	2	(h)	Everton	W	2-0	Parker, Gaynor	26,008
21		15	(a)	Tottenham H	W	2-1	Parker, Clough	16,903
22		21	(h)	Aston Villa	W	4-0	Hodge, Pearce, Parker, Laws	22,662
23	Feb	4	(a)	Luton T	W	3-2	Parker, Clough 2 (1 pen)	10,465
24		11	(h)	QPR	D	0-0		19,690
25	Mar	11	(a)	Arsenal	W	3-1	Clough, Carr, Pearce	39,639
26		15	(h)	Newcastle U	D	1-1	Clough (pen)	20,800
27		22	(h)	Tottenham H	L	1-2	Parker	23,098
28		25	(a)	Derby Co	W	2-0	Hodge, Chapman	25,174
29		27	(h)	Manchester U	W	2-0	Pearce, Chapman	30,092
30	Apr	1	(a)	Wimbledon	L	1-4	Clough	7,867
31		5	(h)	Norwich C	W	2-0	Clough, Pearce	19,872
32		12	(h)	Southampton	W	3-0	Clough (pen), Pearce, Gaynor	18,948
33		22	(a)	Middlesbrough	W	4-3	Webb, Chapman 2, Parker	20,778
34	May	3	(h)	Millwall	W	4-1	Gaynor, Hodge, Wood (og), Parker	15,928
35		10	(a)	Liverpool	L	0-1		39,793
36		13	(h)	Charlton Ath	W	4-0	Carr, Wilson, Webb, Chettle	17,637
37		15	(a)	Coventry C	D	2-2	Webb, Clough	14,003
38		18	(h)	West Ham U	L	1-2	Chapman	20,843

FINAL LEAGUE POSITION : 3rd in Division One

Appearances

Sub. Appearances

Goals

Sutton	Chettle	Pearce	Walker	Foster	Wilson	Crosby	Webb	Clough	Hodge	Rice	Carr	Gaynor	Chapman	Crossley	Charles	Starbuck	Laws	Parker	Williams	
1	2	3	4	5	6	7	8	9	10	11*	12									1
1	2	3	4	5	6	7	8	9	10	11										2
1	2	3	4	5		7*	8	9	6	11	12	10								3
1	2	3	4	5		7	8	9	6	11	12	10*								4
1	2	3	4	5		7	8	9	6	11	12	10*								5
1	2	3	4	5		7	8	9	6	11	12	10*								6
1	2	3	4	5		11	8	9	6		7	10								7
1	2	3	4	5		7	8	9	6		11	10								8
	2	3	4	5		7	8	9	6	11		10	1							9
	2	3	4	5	12	7	8*	9	6	11		10	1							10
1	2	3	4	5	8			9	6	11		10	7*	12						11
1	2	3†	4	5	8	12		9	6	11		10*	7			14				12
1	2	3	4	5	12	7*	8	9	6	11		10								13
1	2	3	4	5	12		8	9	6	11		10*	7							14
1	2	3	4	5			8	9	6	11	7	10								15
1	4	3		5			8	9		11	7	10					2	6		16
1	2†		4	5			8	9	12	11	7	10				14		6*	3	17
1			4	5			8	9*	6	11	7	14	10†		12		2		3	18
1		3	4	5			8		6		7*	9	10	12			2	11		19
1		3	4	5			8		6		7*	9	10	12			2	11		20
1	12	3	4*	5			8	9	6		7		10				2	11		21
1	4	3		5	12		8	9	6		7*		10				2	11		22
1	4	3		5			8	9	6		7		10				2	11		23
1	4	3		5			8	9	6		7		10*	12			2	11		24
1		3	4	5			8	9	6		7		10				2	11		25
1		3	4	5			8	9	6		7		10				2	11		26
1		3	4	5			8	9	6		7		10				2	11		27
1	12	3	4	5			8	9	6		7*		10				2	11		28
1	12	3*	4	5			8	9	6		7		10				2	11		29
1	2	3	4	5			8	9	6		7		10					11		30
1	2	3	4	5	12		8	9	6		7		10*					11		31
1		3	4	5			8	9*	6	12	7		10				2	11		32
1	12	3	4	5			8	9	6		7*		10				2	11		33
1		3	4	5			8	9	6		7		10				2	11		34
1		3	4	5			8	9	6		7*	12	10				2	11		35
1	14	3	4	5			8	9	6		7	12	10*				2	11†		36
1		3	4	5			8	9	6		7		10				2	11		37
1	5	3	4				8	9	6		7		10				2	11		38
36	23	36	34	17	24	11	36	36	33	19	18	16	30	2	1	2	20	22	2	
	5		1	3	2		1	1	5	3							5	2		
	2	6		2	1		6	14	7	1	3	4	8					1	7	

51

1989-90

1	Aug	19	(h)	Aston Villa	D	1-1	Parker	26,766
2		23	(a)	Norwich C	D	1-1	Chapman	18,267
3		26	(a)	Millwall	L	0-1		12,140
4		30	(h)	Derby Co	W	2-1	Crosby, Pearce	24,060
5	Sep	9	(a)	Chelsea	D	2-2	Chapman 2	21,523
6		16	(h)	Arsenal	L	1-2	Parker	22,216
7		23	(a)	Crystal Palace	L	0-1		12,899
8		30	(h)	Charlton Ath	W	2-0	Laws, Chapman	18,189
9	Oct	14	(a)	Coventry C	W	2-0	Crosby, Rice	15,722
10		21	(a)	Wimbledon	W	3-1	Hodge, Parker, Pearce (pen)	5,184
11		28	(h)	QPR	D	2-2	Crosby, Chapman	19,442
12	Nov	4	(h)	Sheffield W	L	0-1		21,864
13		12	(a)	Manchester U	L	0-1		34,182
14		18	(a)	Manchester C	W	3-0	Clough 2 (1 pen), Rice	26,238
15		25	(h)	Everton	W	1-0	Clough (pen)	20,709
16	Dec	2	(a)	Aston Villa	L	1-2	Chapman	25,575
17		9	(h)	Norwich C	L	0-1		18,939
18		17	(h)	Southampton	W	2-0	Hodge, Chapman	16,437
19		26	(a)	Luton T	D	1-1	Hodge	10,754
20		30	(a)	Tottenham H	W	3-2	Clough, Crosby, Parker	33,401
21	Jan	1	(h)	Liverpool	D	2-2	Hodge, Clough (pen)	24,518
22		13	(h)	Millwall	W	3-1	Clough, Laws, Hodge	18,065
23		20	(a)	Derby Co	W	2-0	Hodge, Jemson	24,176
24	Feb	3	(h)	Crystal Palace	W	3-1	Clough, Hodge, Jemson	19,739
25		17	(h)	Chelsea	D	1-1	Orlygsson	22,500
26	Mar	3	(h)	Manchester C	W	1-0	Crosby	22,644
27		7	(a)	Arsenal	L	0-3		31,879
28		10	(h)	Coventry C	L	2-4	Currie, Laws	18,750
29		17	(a)	Charlton Ath	D	1-1	Hodge	6,690
30		24	(a)	QPR	L	0-2		14,653
31		31	(h)	Wimbledon	L	0-1		16,821
32	Apr	4	(a)	Everton	L	0-4		17,795
33		7	(h)	Tottenham H	L	1-3	Hodge	21,669
34		14	(a)	Liverpool	D	2-2	Hodge, Jemson	37,265
35		16	(h)	Luton T	W	3-0	Carr, Parker, Clough	17,001
36		21	(a)	Southampton	L	0-2		17,006
37	May	2	(h)	Manchester U	W	4-0	Parker, Pearce, Clough, Chettle	21,186
38		5	(a)	Sheffield W	W	3-0	Pearce 2, Jemson	29,762

FINAL LEAGUE POSITION : 9th in Division One

Appearances

Sub. Appearances

Goals

52

Sutton	Laws	Pearce	Walker	Foster	Hodge	Carr	Parker	Clough	Chapman	Crosby	Rice	Wilson	Gaynor	Starbuck	Chettle	Wassall	Crossley	Orlygsson	Jemson	Charles	Currie	Williams	No.
1	2	3	4	5	6	7	8	9	10	11													1
1	2	3	4	5	6	7	8	9	10	11													2
1	2	3	4	5	6	7*	8	9	10	11	12												3
1	2	3	4	5	6		8	9	10	7	11												4
1	2	3	4	5	6*		8	9	10	7	11	12											5
1	2	3	4	5	6		11	9	10*	7		8†	12	14									6
1	2		4		6		8	9	10	7	11*	5	12		3								7
1	2		4		6	7	8	9	10		11*		12	3	5								8
1	2	3	4		6		8	9	10	7	11	5											9
1	2	3	4		6		8	9*	10	7		5		12	11								10
1	2	3	4		6*		8	9	10	7	12	5	11										11
1	2	3	4		6	12	8	9	10	7		5	11*										12
	2	3	4		6		8	9	10	7	11	5*		12			1						13
	2	3	4		6		8	9	10	7	11			5			1						14
	2	3	4		6		8	9	10	7	11			5			1						15
	2	3	4		6		8	9	10	7	11			5			1						16
1	2	3	4		6		8	9	10	7	11			5									17
1	2	3	4		6			9	10	7	11			5			8						18
1	2	3	4		6		8	9		7				5			11	10					19
1	2	3	4		6		8	9		7*				5			11	10	12				20
1	2	3	4		6		8	9		7				5			11	10					21
1	2	3	4		6*		8	9		7	12			5			11	10					22
1	2	3	4		6		8	9		7				5			11	10*	12				23
1	2	3	4		6		8	9		7				5			11*	10	12				24
1	2	3	4		6		8	9		7	5						11	10					25
1	2	3	4		6		8	9		7		12		5*			11	10					26
1	2	3	4				8	9		7	6	5					11	10					27
1	2	3	4				8†	9		7	6	5	14				11*	10	12				28
1	2	3	4		6		8*	9		7	12	5	14					11			10†		29
1	2†	3	4			7	8*	9			6	5	11					14	10		12		30
1	2	3	4			11	8	9		7	6	5							10				31
1	2		4		6	12	14	9		7	11	8†		5					10*	3			32
1	2		4		6	11	8	9		7		5		3				10					33
	2	3	4		6	7	11	9				8		5		1		10					34
	2	3	4		6	7	11	9				8		5		1		10					35
	2	3	4		6*	7	11	9				8†	14	5		1		10	12				36
	2	3	4		6	12	8	9		7			11	5†	14	1		10*					37
1	2	3	4		6	12	8	9		7			11*		5			10					38
30	38	34	38	6	34	10	36	38	18	34	15	18	5	21	2	8	11	17	4	1			
						4	1					3	3	6	2	1	1		1	1	1	4	
	3	5			10	1	6	9	7	5	2				1			1	4		1		

53

1990-91

1	Aug	25	(h)	QPR	D	1-1	Jemson (pen)	21,619
2		28	(a)	Liverpool	L	0-2		33,663
3	Sep	1	(a)	Coventry C	D	2-2	Jemson 2 (1 pen)	12,630
4		8	(h)	Southampton	W	3-1	Wilson, Jemson 2	18,559
5		15	(a)	Crystal Palace	D	2-2	Pearce 2	20,545
6		22	(h)	Arsenal	L	0-2		26,013
7		29	(a)	Manchester U	W	1-0	Pearce	46,766
8	Oct	7	(h)	Everton	W	3-1	Hodge 2, Jemson	25,790
9		20	(a)	Chelsea	D	0-0		22,403
10		27	(h)	Tottenham H	L	1-2	Clough	27,347
11	Nov	3	(a)	Leeds U	L	1-3	Jemson	30,409
12		10	(a)	Aston Villa	D	1-1	Carr	25,797
13		17	(h)	Sunderland	W	2-0	Chettle, Clough	22,757
14		24	(a)	Derby Co	L	1-2	Chettle	21,723
15	Dec	1	(h)	Luton T	D	2-2	Carr, Clough	16,498
16		15	(a)	QPR	W	2-1	Clough, Pearce	10,156
17		22	(a)	Sheffield U	L	2-3	Keane, Pearce	20,394
18		26	(h)	Wimbledon	W	2-1	Pearce, Keane	16,221
19		29	(h)	Manchester C	L	1-3	Gaynor	24,937
20	Jan	2	(a)	Norwich C	W	6-2	Wilson, Clough, Polston (og), Keane 2, Crosby	17,043
21		12	(h)	Coventry C	W	3-0	Pearce, Clough, Keane	18,344
22		19	(a)	Southampton	D	1-1	Clough	16,044
23	Feb	2	(h)	Crystal Palace	L	0-1		17,045
24		16	(a)	Sunderland	L	0-1		20,394
25		23	(h)	Aston Villa	D	2-2	Clough, Hodge	22,036
26	Mar	2	(a)	Luton T	L	0-1		9,577
27		16	(h)	Manchester U	D	1-1	Wilson	23,859
28		20	(a)	Arsenal	D	1-1	Jemson	34,152
29		23	(a)	Everton	D	0-0		23,078
30		30	(a)	Wimbledon	L	1-3	Loughlan	6,392
31	Apr	1	(h)	Sheffield U	W	2-0	Gaynor 2	25,308
32		6	(a)	Manchester C	L	1-3	Pearce	25,169
33		10	(h)	Derby Co	W	1-0	Keane	25,109
34		20	(h)	Chelsea	W	7-0	Keane 2, Parker, Woan, Clough, Pearce 2	20,305
35		24	(h)	Norwich C	W	5-0	Glover, Clough, Pearce, Crosby, Woan	17,641
36	May	4	(a)	Tottenham H	D	1-1	Clough	30,891
37		6	(h)	Liverpool	W	2-1	Clough (pen), Woan	26,151
38		11	(h)	Leeds U	W	4-3	Parker 2, Clough 2	25,067

FINAL LEAGUE POSITION : 8th in Division One

Appearances

Sub. Appearances

Goals

Crossley	Laws	Williams	Walker	Chettle	Hodge	Crosby	Parker	Clough	Jemson	Carr	Wassall	Keane	Starbuck	Wilson	Pearce	Gaynor	Rice	Charles	Woan	Loughlan	Glover	Gemmill	
1	2	3	4	5*	6	7	8	9	10	11	12												1
1	2	3	4	5		7	8	9	10			6	11										2
1	2	3	4	5	6*		8	9	10	11		7		12									3
1	2*		4	5		8	9	10	7	12	11†			6	3	14							4
1	2		4	5		8	9	10		7				6	3	11*	12						5
1	2		4	5		7	8	9	10			6			3	11							6
1	2		4	5		7	8	9	10			6			3	11							7
1	2		4	5	6	7	8	9*	10			11			3	12							8
1	2		4	5	6	10	12	9	7			11		8*	3								9
1	2		4	5	6	7	8	9	10			11			3								10
1	2			5		7	8*	9	10	4	6	12			3	11†	14						11
1	2		4	5		7	8	9	10	11		6			3								12
1	2		4	5	6*	7	11	9	10			8	12		3								13
1	2		4	5	6*	7	11	9	10			8	12		3								14
1	2		4	5		11	8	9	10*	7		6	12		3								15
1	2		4	5		11	8	9	10	7		6			3								16
1	2		4	5		11	8	9	10*	7		6	12		3								17
1	2		4	5	6†	11	9	10*	7			8	12	14	3								18
1	2		4	5		14	11†	9	7			8*	12	6	3	10							19
1	2		4	5		11	10	9		7		8		6*	3				12				20
1	2		4	5		10	11	9	7*	14	6	12	8†		3								21
1	2	3	4	5	12	10	11	9	7*			6	8										22
1			4	5	6	7	11	9				10		8	3			2					23
1	2		4	5	12	14	11	9	10	7†		8			3	6*							24
1	2		4	5	6	7	11*	9				10		8	3			12					25
1			4	5		6	9	10		7				8	3			2	11				26
1	2		4	5		7	11	9	10			6		8	3								27
1	2		4	5		7	11	9	10			6		8	3								28
1	3		4			7	11	9	10			5		6		12	8*	2					29
1			4	5		11	9					8†		6	3*			2	12	7	10	14	30
1			4	5		8	9							6	3	10		2	11	7			31
1			4	5		9								6	3	7		2	11		10	8	32
1	12		4	5		9								6	3	7*		2	11		10	8	33
1	12		4	5		7	8	9						6	3			2	11		10		34
1	12		4	5		7	8	9†						6	3			2*	11		10	14	35
1	2		4	5		7	8	9				12		6*	3				11		10		36
1	2		4	5	6	7	8	9							3				11		10		37
1	2		4	5	6	7	8	9	12						3*				11		10		38
38	30	4	37	37	12	27	35	37	22	13	3	35	3	13	33	9	9	9	2	8	2		
	2			2	2	1		1	4					9	2		2	1	1	3	2		
			2	3	2	3	14	8	2			8		3	11	3		3	1	1			

1991-92

1	Aug	17	(h)	Everton	W	2-1	Clough, Jemson	24,422
2		20	(a)	Leeds U	L	0-1		29,457
3		24	(a)	Notts Co	W	4-0	Crosby, Charles, Sheringham, Keane	21,044
4		28	(h)	Tottenham H	L	1-3	Clough	24,018
5		31	(h)	Oldham Ath	W	3-1	Gemmill, Keane, Pearce	23,244
6	Sep	4	(a)	Manchester C	L	1-2	Sheringham	29,146
7		7	(a)	Sheffield W	L	1-2	Crosby	31,289
8		14	(h)	Wimbledon	W	4-2	Keane 2, Black, Elkins (og)	19,707
9		21	(a)	Aston Villa	L	1-3	Teale (og)	28,506
10		28	(h)	West Ham U	D	2-2	Woan, Sheringham	25,613
11	Oct	5	(a)	QPR	W	2-0	Sheringham 2	13,508
12		19	(a)	Sheffield U	L	2-4	Parker, Chettle	23,080
13		26	(h)	Southampton	L	1-3	Black	20,026
14	Nov	2	(a)	Norwich C	D	0-0		13,014
15		16	(h)	Coventry C	W	1-0	Sheringham	21,154
16		23	(h)	Crystal Palace	W	5-1	Sheringham 2 (1 pen), Pearce, Gemmill, Woan	22,387
17		30	(a)	Chelsea	L	0-1		19,420
18	Dec	8	(h)	Arsenal	W	3-2	Woan, Sheringham, Gemmill	22,095
19		13	(a)	Liverpool	L	0-2		35,285
20		22	(h)	Leeds U	D	0-0		27,170
21		26	(a)	Tottenham H	W	2-1	Clough, Pearce	31,079
22		28	(a)	Oldham Ath	L	1-2	Pearce	16,496
23	Jan	1	(h)	Luton T	D	1-1	Walker	23,809
24		11	(h)	Notts Co	D	1-1	Black	30,168
25		19	(a)	Everton	D	1-1	Gemmill	17,717
26	Feb	1	(h)	Sheffield U	L	2-5	Keane, Pearce (pen)	22,412
27		22	(h)	Chelsea	D	1-1	Sheringham	24,095
28	Mar	3	(a)	Crystal Palace	D	0-0		12,608
29		11	(a)	Coventry C	W	2-0	Smith (og), Sheringham	11,158
30		14	(h)	Norwich C	W	2-0	Keane, Gemmill	20,721
31		18	(h)	Manchester U	W	1-0	Clough	28,062
32		21	(h)	Manchester C	W	2-0	Crosby, Keane	24,115
33		31	(a)	Arsenal	D	3-3	Woan, Clough, Keane	27,036
34	Apr	2	(a)	Wimbledon	L	0-3		3,542
35		4	(h)	Sheffield W	L	0-2		26,105
36		8	(a)	Southampton	W	1-0	Tiler	14,905
37		14	(a)	Luton T	L	1-2	Black	8,014
38		18	(h)	Aston Villa	W	2-0	Gemmill, Sheringham	22,800
39		20	(a)	Manchester U	W	2-1	Woan, Gemmill	47,576
40		22	(h)	Liverpool	D	1-1	Sheringham (pen)	23,787
41		25	(h)	QPR	D	1-1	Gemmill	22,228
42	May	2	(a)	West Ham U	L	0-3		20,629

FINAL LEAGUE POSITION : 8th in Division One

Appearances

Sub. Appearances

Goals

Crossley	Charles	Pearce	Walker	Tiler	Keane	Crosby	Gemmill	Clough	Sheringham	Jemson	Chettle	Laws	Black	Williams	Parker	Gaynor	Woan	Wassall	Glover	Marriott	Ortysson	Kaminsky	Wilson	Stone	#
1	2	3	4*	5	6	7	8	9	10	11	12														1
1	2	3		5	6	7	8	9	10	11	4														2
1	2	3		5	6	7	8	9	10	11*	4	12													3
1	2	3		5	6	7	8	9	10	11	4														4
1	2	3		5	6	7	8	9	10	11	4														5
1	2	3		5	6	7	8	9	10	11*	4	12													6
1	2	3		5	6	7	8	9	10		4		11												7
1	2			5	6	7	8	9	10		4		11	3											8
1	2			5	6	7	8*	9†	10		4	14	11	3	12										9
1	2	3	12	5	6				10		4	7					8	9*	11						10
1	2	3	4	5	6	7			10			12	11				8	9*							11
1	2	3	4	5	6*	7			10			12	11†				8	9	14						12
1		3	4*	5		7	8		9			2	12	11			10		6						13
1	2	3	4		6	7	8		10		5		11	8					9						14
1	2	3	4		6	7	8		10		5		11						9						15
1	2	3	4		6†	7*	8	12	10		5		11	14					9						16
1	2	3	4		6*		8	9	10		5		11	12	7										17
1	2	3	4	5	6	7	8	9	10				11												18
1	2	3	4	12	6	7	8	9	10*		5		11												19
1	2	3	4	5	6		8	9	10			7*	11						12						20
1	2	3	4	5	6*		8	9	10			7	11	12											21
1	2	3	4	5	6		8	9	10*			7	11						12						22
1	2	3	4	5	6	7	8	9	10			11													23
1	2*	3	4	5†	6	12	8		10			7	11	14	9										24
1		3	4		6		8		10	12	2	7					11	5*	9						25
1		3	4	5	6	12	8	9			2	7*					11		10						26
1		3	4		6	7	8	9	10		2	11					5								27
1	2	3	4	5	6		8	9	10							7	11								28
1	2	3	4		6	7	8	9	10							5	11								29
1	2	3	4	5	6	7	8	9	10			11													30
	2	3	4		6	7	8	9	10			11					5		1						31
	2*	3	4		6	7	8	9	10		12	14					5		1						32
	2		4		6		8	9	10		3	7				11	5		1						33
	2†		4	14	6		8	9		3*	12	7				11	5	10	1						34
			4	5	6	7	8	9		2		3				11		10	1						35
			4*	11	6	7	8	9	10	2		3				5	12	1							36
1			4*		6	7	8	9	10		11	3				5		2	12						37
1				6	5	8	9	10		2	7	3	11					4							38
1		4		6	5	8	9	10		2		3	11					7							39
1		4		6	5	8	9	10		2		3	11					7							40
1		4		6	5	8	9	10		2	11		12	3		7*									41
1		4			5	8	9	10		2	7	3	11*		12					6†	14				42
36	30	30	32	24	39	31	39	33	39	6	17	10	25	9	5	3	20	10	12	6	5	1			
			1	2		2	1					5	5				1	1	1	4	4		1	1	
	1	5	1	1	8	3	8	5	13	1	1		4				1		5						

1992-93

#	Month	Date		Opponent	Result	Score	Scorers	Attendance
1	Aug	16	(h)	Liverpool	W	1-0	Sheringham	20,038
2		19	(a)	Sheffield W	L	0-2		29,623
3		22	(a)	Oldham Ath	L	3-5	Pearce (pen), Bannister 2	11,632
4		29	(h)	Manchester U	L	0-2		19,694
5		31	(a)	Norwich C	L	1-3	Clough	14,104
6	Sep	5	(a)	Blackburn R	L	1-4	Bannister	16,180
7		12	(h)	Sheffield W	L	1-2	Bannister	19,420
8		21	(h)	Coventry C	D	1-1	Clough	17,553
9		26	(a)	Chelsea	D	0-0		19,760
10	Oct	3	(a)	Manchester C	D	2-2	McKinnon, Pearce	22,571
11		17	(h)	Arsenal	L	0-1		24,862
12		21	(h)	Middlesbrough	W	1-0	Black	17,846
13		24	(a)	Sheffield U	D	0-0		19,152
14		31	(h)	Ipswich T	L	0-1		21,411
15	Nov	7	(h)	Everton	L	0-1		20,941
16		21	(a)	Crystal Palace	D	1-1	Bannister	15,330
17		28	(h)	Southampton	L	1-2	Clough	19,942
18	Dec	5	(a)	Leeds U	W	4-1	Clough, Keane 2, Black	29,364
19		12	(a)	Aston Villa	L	1-2	Keane	29,015
20		20	(h)	Wimbledon	D	1-1	Clough	19,326
21		28	(a)	Tottenham H	L	1-2	Gemmill	32,118
22	Jan	9	(a)	Coventry C	W	1-0	Woan	15,264
23		16	(h)	Chelsea	W	3-0	Bannister 2, Orlygsson	23,249
24		27	(a)	Manchester U	L	0-2		36,085
25		30	(h)	Oldham Ath	W	2-0	Woan 2	21,240
26	Feb	6	(a)	Liverpool	D	0-0		40,463
27		20	(a)	Middlesbrough	W	2-1	Clough, Stone	15,639
28		24	(h)	QPR	W	1-0	Crosby	22,436
29		27	(h)	Manchester C	L	0-2		25,956
30	Mar	3	(h)	Crystal Palace	D	1-1	Keane	20,603
31		13	(a)	Everton	L	0-3		21,271
32		17	(h)	Norwich C	L	0-3		20,799
33		21	(h)	Leeds U	D	1-1	Clough (pen)	25,148
34		24	(a)	Southampton	W	2-1	Clough, Keane	18,005
35	Apr	4	(h)	Aston Villa	L	0-1		26,742
36		7	(h)	Blackburn R	L	1-3	Clough (pen)	20,467
37		10	(a)	QPR	L	3-4	Bannister, Black 2	15,815
38		12	(h)	Tottenham H	W	2-1	Black, Rosario	25,682
39		17	(a)	Wimbledon	L	0-1		9,358
40		21	(a)	Arsenal	D	1-1	Keane	19,024
41	May	1	(h)	Sheffield U	L	0-2		26,752
42		8	(a)	Ipswich T	L	1-2	Clough (pen)	22,093

FINAL LEAGUE POSITION : 22nd in Premier League

Appearances

Sub. Appearances

Goals

Crossley	Laws	Pearce	Wilson	Chettle	Keane	Crosby	Gemmill	Clough	Sheringham	Woan	Black	Bannister	Orlygsson	Tiler	McKinnon	Charles	Glover	Webb	Williams	Stone	Rosario	Marriott	#
1	2	3	4	5	6	7*	8	9	10	11	12												1
1	2	3	4	5	6	7	8	9	10	11													2
1	2	3	4*	5	6	7	8	9	10†	11	12	14											3
1	2	3	4	5	6	7	8			11	10												4
1	2	3	4	5	6		8	9		11	10	7											5
1	2	3		5	6	11	8	9			10	7	4										6
1	2	3		5	6*	7	8	9		11	10		4	12									7
1	2	3			6	7	8	9			10	11	5	4									8
1	2	3			6	7	8	9			10	11	5	4									9
1	2	3			6	7	8	9			10	11	5	4									10
1		3			6	7	8	9		12	10	11	5	4*	2								11
1		3	4			7	8	9		11	10*	6	5		2	12							12
1		3	4			7	8	9		11		6	5		2	10							13
1	2	3	4			7	8	9		11	12	6*	5			10							14
1	2	3	4		6		8	9		11		7	5			10							15
1	2	3	4		6		8	9		11		7	5			10							16
1	2	3	4		6		8	9		11		7*	5			12	10						17
1	2	3	4		6		8	9		11	12	14	5			10†	7						18
1	2	3	4		6		8	9		11		12	5			10*	7						19
1	2	3	4		6	7	8	9		11			5			10							20
1	2	3	4		6	7	8	9		12	11*		5			10							21
1	2	3	4		6		8	9		11		7	5			10							22
1	2	3	4		6		8*	9		11		7	12	5		10							23
1	2		4		6†	14	8	9		11	*	7	12	5		10				3			24
1	2		4		6		8	9		11		7		5		10				3			25
1	2		4		6		8	9		11		7	10	5						3			26
1		3			6		8	9		11		10	7	5	2				4				27
1		3			6	7	8	9		11		10		5	2				4				28
1	12	3			6	7		9		11	8			5	2	10			4*				29
1		3	4		6	7		9		11	12	8*		5	2						10		30
1		3	4		7*			9		11	10	6		5	8	2	12						31
1		3	4		7*			9		11	12	10†	6	5	2	14	8						32
1		3			6			9		11	7	8		5		2			4		10		33
1	3*				6	12		9		11	7	8		5		2			4		10		34
1		3			6	12		9		11	7	8		5		2			4		10*		35
1		3			6		8	9		11	7			5		2			4		10		36
1					6	11		9			7	8		5		2			4	3	10		37
	2				6			9		11	7	8	12	5					4	3	10*	1	38
	2				6			9		11	7*	8		5		12			4	3	10	1	39
	2				6		8	9		11	7			5		12			4	3	10*	1	40
	2		4		6		8	9		11	7			5						3	10	1	41
	2		4		6		8	9		11	7*	12		5		10				3		1	42
37	32	23	5	30	40	20	33	42	3	27	19	27	15	37	5	14	9	9	9	11	10	5	
	1				3			1	5	4	5		1		5					1			
	2		6	1	1	10	1	3	5	8	1	1			1					1	1		

1993-94

1	Aug	15	(a)	Southend U	D	1-1	Pearce (pen)	8,609
2		18	(h)	Derby Co	D	1-1	Woan	26,682
3		21	(h)	Grimsby T	W	5-3	Black, Futcher (og), Glover, Woan, Rosario	23,225
4		24	(a)	Crystal Palace	L	0-2		15,048
5		28	(a)	Luton T	W	2-1	Black, Woan	9,788
6	Sep	11	(a)	Barnsley	L	0-1		13,280
7		19	(h)	Stoke C	L	2-3	Phillips, Pearce	20,843
8		26	(a)	Bolton W	L	3-4	Collymore 2, Phillips	10,578
9	Oct	2	(h)	Portsmouth	D	1-1	Stone	20,727
10		16	(h)	Tranmere R	W	2-1	Collymore, Gemmill	20,771
11		20	(h)	Oxford U	D	0-0		18,462
12		24	(a)	Leicester C	L	0-1		17,624
13		30	(h)	Notts Co	W	1-0	Collymore	26,721
14	Nov	3	(h)	Millwall	L	1-3	Glover	17,584
15		6	(a)	Birmingham C	W	3-0	Collymore, Glover 2	16,996
16		10	(a)	Wolverhampton W	D	1-1	Collymore	21,621
17		21	(a)	West Brom A	W	2-0	Collymore 2	15,581
18		27	(a)	Sunderland	W	3-2	Gemmill, Collymore 2	16,968
19	Dec	4	(h)	Birmingham C	W	1-0	Whyte (og)	22,061
20		19	(h)	Southend U	W	2-0	Cooper, Black	21,641
21		27	(h)	Middlesbrough	D	1-1	Collymore	26,901
22		28	(a)	Bristol C	W	4-1	Collymore 2, Webb, Woan	20,725
23	Jan	1	(h)	Charlton Ath	D	1-1	Lyttle	26,543
24		3	(a)	Watford	W	2-1	Cooper, Gemmill	14,539
25		16	(a)	Tranmere R	W	2-1	Cooper, Gemmill	8,500
26		23	(h)	Wolverhampton W	D	0-0		23,008
27	Feb	6	(h)	Leicester C	W	4-0	Gemmill 2, Glover, Woan	26,616
28		12	(a)	Notts Co	L	1-2	Phillips	18,655
29		19	(h)	Crystal Palace	D	1-1	Bohinen	24,232
30		25	(a)	Oxford U	L	0-1		9,346
31	Mar	2	(h)	Peterborough U	W	2-0	Gemmill 2	19,329
32		5	(h)	Luton T	W	2-0	Cooper, Pearce (pen)	22,249
33		12	(a)	Stoke C	W	1-0	Webb	20,550
34		16	(h)	Barnsley	W	2-1	Cooper, Phillips	20,491
35		19	(h)	Bolton W	W	3-2	Chettle, Pearce, Collymore	23,846
36		26	(a)	Portsmouth	L	1-2	Collymore	12,578
37		30	(h)	Watford	W	2-1	Stone, Webb	23,044
38	Apr	2	(a)	Middlesbrough	D	2-2	Lee, Rosario	17,056
39		4	(h)	Bristol C	D	0-0		24,162
40		9	(a)	Charlton Ath	W	1-0	Lee	12,330
41		17	(a)	Millwall	D	2-2	Collymore, Stone	12,543
42		24	(h)	West Brom A	W	2-1	Stone, Cooper	24,018
43		27	(a)	Derby Co	W	2-0	Cooper, Stone	19,300
44		30	(a)	Peterborough U	W	3-2	Collymore 2, Pearce	14,010
45	May	3	(a)	Grimsby T	D	0-0		11,930
46		8	(h)	Sunderland	D	2-2	Pearce (pen), Collymore	27,010

FINAL LEAGUE POSITION : 2nd in Division One

Appearances

Sub. Appearances

Goals

Crossley	Lyttle	Pearce	Cooper	Chetle	Stone	Black	Webb	Rosario	Glover	Woan	Harvey	Laws	Phillips	Collymore	Warner	Blatherwick	Gemmill	Wright	Kilford	Howe	Crosby	Bohinen	Bull	Haaland	Lee	Tiler	
1	2	3	4	5	6	7	8	9	10†	11*	12	14															1
1	2	3	4	5	6	7	8	9	10*	11	12																2
1	2	3	4	5	6	7	8	9	10	11*			12														3
1	2	3	4	5	6*	7	8	9	14	11			12	10†													4
1	2	3		5	6	7*	8	9	10	11			12			4											5
1	2	3		5	6	7*	8	9	12	11				10		4											6
1	2	3		5	6		9*	8		11			7	10		4	12										7
	2			5		7		9*		11†			3	6	10	4	8	1		12		14					8
		3		5	6	11						2	7	10			8	1				9	4				9
		3		5	6	11		9*				2	7	10			8	1				12	4				10
		3	12	5	6	11		9				2	7				8	1				10*	4				11
		3	4†	5	6	11	12	9*				2	7	10			8	1				14					12
		3	4	5	6	11		9				2	7	10			8	1									13
	2	3	4	5	6	11	12	9					7	10			8*	1									14
	2		4	5	6	11	12	9					7	10			8	1						3*			15
	2	3	4	5	6			9					7	10			8	1				11					16
1	2	3	4	5	6	11							7	10			8					9					17
12	2	3	4	5	6	11							7	10			8	1*				9					18
1		3	4	5	6	11	12					2		10			8				7*	9					19
1	2	3	4	5	6	11							7	10			8					9					20
1	2	3	4	5	6	11							7	10			8					9					21
1	2		4	5	6	3	11						7	10			8					9					22
1	2	3	4	5	6*	12	8			11			7	10								9					23
1	2	3	4	5	6	12	9			11*			7	10†			8					14					24
1	2	3	4	5	6†	12	9		10	11*			7				8					14					25
1		3	4	5	6	8			10	11			7	2								9*			12		26
1	2	3		5	6				10	11			7				8				4	9					27
1	2	3	4	5	6*	11			10				7				8					9			12		28
1	2	3	4	5	6				10	11*			7				8					9			12		29
1	2	3	4	5	6				10	11*			7				8					9			12		30
1	2	3	4	5	6	11							7				8					9			10		31
1	2	3	4	5	6	11	12						7				8					9*			10		32
1	2	3	4	5	6	11			10				7				8					9					33
1	2	3	4	5	6	11	8						7									9		12	10*		34
1	2	3		5	6†	11	8						7				12				14	9*	4		10		35
1	2†	3	4	5	6	11	8		14				7	10								9*			12		36
1		3	4	5	6	11	8						7	10										2	9		37
1	2	3	4	5	6	11	8*	9					7									12			10		38
1	2	3	4	5	6	11			10	12			7				8*					9					39
1	2	3	4	5	6	11	8	9*					7									12			10		40
1	2	3		5	6	11							7	10			8				4	9					41
1	2	3*	4	5	6	12	11						7	10			8					9					42
1	2	3	4	5	6	11							7	10			8					9					43
1	2	3	4	5	6	12		9†		11			7	10			8					14					44
1		3	4	5	6*	12	11						7	10			8					9†			14	2	45
1		3	4	5	6	12	11						7	10			8					9*				2	46
36	37	42	36	46	45	30	17	15	15	23		6	40	27	1	3	30	10		2	4	22	3	3	10	3	
1		1				7	4	1	3	1	2	1	3	1		1			1		1	2	2	1	8	3	
	1	6	7	1	5	3	3	2	5	5			4	19			8					1			2		

1994-95

1	Aug	20	(a)	Ipswich T	W	1-0	Roy	18,763
2		22	(h)	Manchester U	D	1-1	Collymore	22,072
3		27	(h)	Leicester C	W	1-0	Collymore	21,601
4		30	(a)	Everton	W	2-1	Hinchcliffe (og), Cooper	26,689
5	Sep	10	(h)	Sheffield W	W	4-1	Black, Bohinen, Pearce (pen), Roy	22,022
6		17	(a)	Southampton	D	1-1	Collymore	14,185
7		24	(a)	Tottenham H	W	4-1	Stone, Roy 2, Bohinen	24,558
8	Oct	2	(h)	QPR	W	3-2	Black, Roy, Collymore	21,449
9		8	(a)	Manchester C	D	3-3	Collymore, Dibble (og), Woan	23,150
10		17	(h)	Wimbledon	W	3-1	Bohinen, Collymore, Woan	20,287
11		22	(a)	Aston Villa	W	2-0	Pearce (pen), Stone	29,217
12		29	(h)	Blackburn R	L	0-2		22,131
13	Nov	5	(a)	Liverpool	L	0-1		33,329
14		7	(h)	Newcastle U	D	0-0		22,102
15		19	(h)	Chelsea	L	0-1		22,092
16		26	(a)	Leeds U	L	0-1		37,709
17	Dec	3	(h)	Arsenal	D	2-2	Pearce (pen), Roy	21,662
18		10	(h)	Ipswich T	W	4-1	Collymore, Gemmill, Haaland, Pearce	21,340
19		17	(a)	Manchester U	W	2-1	Collymore, Pearce	43,744
20		26	(a)	Coventry C	D	0-0		19,116
21		27	(h)	Norwich C	W	1-0	Bohinen	21,010
22		31	(a)	West Ham U	L	1-3	McGregor	20,644
23	Jan	2	(h)	Crystal Palace	W	1-0	Bull	21,326
24		14	(a)	Blackburn R	L	0-3		27,510
25		21	(h)	Aston Villa	L	1-2	Collymore (pen)	24,598
26		25	(a)	Chelsea	W	2-0	Collymore 2	17,890
27	Feb	4	(h)	Liverpool	D	1-1	Collymore	25,418
28		11	(a)	Newcastle U	L	1-2	Lee	34,471
29		21	(a)	Arsenal	L	0-1		35,441
30		26	(a)	QPR	D	1-1	Stone	13,363
31	Mar	4	(h)	Tottenham H	D	2-2	Bohinen, Lee	28,711
32		8	(h)	Everton	W	2-1	Collymore, Pearce	24,526
33		11	(a)	Leicester C	W	4-2	Pearce (pen), Collymore, Woan, Lee	20,423
34		18	(h)	Southampton	W	3-0	Roy 2, Collymore	24,146
35		22	(h)	Leeds U	W	3-0	Roy 2, Collymore	26,299
36	Apr	1	(a)	Sheffield W	W	7-1	Pearce, Woan, Roy 2, Collymore 2, Bohinen	30,060
37		8	(h)	West Ham U	D	1-1	Collymore	28,361
38		12	(a)	Norwich C	W	1-0	Stone	19,005
39		17	(h)	Coventry C	W	2-0	Woan, Collymore	26,253
40		29	(a)	Crystal Palace	W	2-1	Roy, Collymore	16,335
41	May	6	(h)	Manchester C	W	1-0	Collymore	28,882
42		13	(a)	Wimbledon	D	2-2	Phillips, Stone	15,341

FINAL LEAGUE POSITION : 3rd in F.A. Carling Premiership

Appearances

Sub. Appearances

Goals

62

Crossley	Lyttle	Pearce	Cooper	Chettle	Stone	Phillips	Gemmill	Lee	Woan	Roy	Bohinen	Rosario	Collymore	Black	Haaland	McGregor	Warner	Bull	Tiler	#
1	2	3	4	5	6*	7	8	9	10	11†	12	14								1
1	2	3	4	5	6	7	8			11	9*	12	10							2
1	2	3	4	5	6	7	8			11	9		10							3
1	2	3	4	5	6	7	8*			11	9	12	10							4
1	2	3	4	5	6	7				8	9		10	11						5
1	2	3	4		6	7				8	9		10	11	5					6
1	2	3	4	5	6	7				8	9*		10	11	12					7
1	2	3	4	5	6	7				8	9		10	11						8
1		3	4	5	6	7	8*	12	14			9	10	11†	2					9
1		3	4	5	6	7				11	8	9	10		2					10
1		3	4	5	6	7			12	11	8*	9	10		2					11
1	2	3	4	5	6	7			10	11*	8	9			12					12
1	2	3	4	5	6	7			10	11	8	9								13
1	2	3	4	5	6	7				11*	8	9	10	12						14
1	2	3	4	5	6	7			12	11	8	9*	10							15
1	2	3	4	5	6	7			12	11	8*	9	10							16
1	2	3		5	4	7				11	8	9*	10	12	6					17
1	2	3		5	6	7			12	11	8*	9†	10	4	14					18
1	2	3		5	6	7	8			11	9*	12	10	4						19
1	2	3	4	5	6	7	8†			11		9	10		12	14				20
1	2	3	4	5	6					11*	8	9	10	12	7					21
1	2	3	4†	5	6					11	8	9*	10	12	7	14				22
1	2	3		5	6		8*			11			10	7	12		4	9		23
1	2			5	6	7	8*			11		9	10	3	12				4	24
1	2			5	6	7				11	8	9	10	3					4	25
1	2			5	6	7	8			11*		9	10	4	12				3	26
1	2		4	5	6	3	8		12	11		9*	10		7					27
1	2	3	4	5	6	7	8		12	11			10		9*					28
1	2	3	4	5	6	7	8		10	11*		9				12				29
1	2		4	5	6	3	8*		12	11		9	10		7					30
1	2		4	5	6	3			12	11	8*	9	10		7					31
1	2	3	4	5	6	7			12	11	8*	9	10							32
1	2	3	4	5	6	7			12	11	8*	9	10							33
1		3	4	5	6	7			12	11	8*	9	10		2					34
1	2†	3	4	5	6	7			12	11	8	9	10*			14				35
1	2	3	4	5	6	7				11*	8	9	10			12				36
1	2	3	4	5	6	7			12	11*	8	9†	10			14				37
1	2	3	4	5	6	7			12	11	8*	9	10							38
1	2	3	4	5	6	7			12	11†	8*	9	10			14				39
1	2	3	4	5	6	7	8		12	11		9*	10							40
1	2	3	4	5	6	7	8		12	11		9*	10							41
1	2	3	4	5	6	7	8	9	11				10							42
42	38	36	35	41	41	38	19	5	35	37	30		37	5	18		1	1	3	
							17		2			4	1	5	2	11				
	8	1			5	1	1	3	5	13	6		22	2	1	1		1		

F.A. CUP COMPETITION

1969/70 SEASON
3rd Round
Jan 3 vs Carlisle United (h) 0-0
Att: 23,419
Replay
Jan 6 vs Carlisle United (a) 1-2
Att: 12,840 McCafferty

1970/71 SEASON
3rd Round
Jan 2 vs Luton Town (h) 1-1
Att: 23,230 McIntosh
Replay
Jan 11 vs Luton Town (a) 4-3
Att: 23,483 Collier, Cormack, Lyons, Rees
4th Round
Jan 23 vs Orient (h) 1-1
Att: 25,349 Moore (pen)
Replay
Jan 25 vs Orient (a) 0-0
Att: 18,591 Abandoned at half-time, ground unfit
Replay
Feb 1 vs Orient (a) 1-0
Att: 18,530 Collier
5th Round
Feb 13 vs Tottenham Hotspur (a) 1-2
Att: 46,366 Moore (pen)

1971/72 SEASON
3rd Round
Jan 15 vs Millwall (a) 1-3
Att: 17,940 Richardson

1972/73 SEASON
3rd Round
Jan 13 vs West Bromwich Albion (a) 1-1
Att: 15,795 Galley
Replay
Jan 22 vs West Bromwich Alb. (h) 0-0 (aet.)
Att: 17,069
2nd Replay
Jan 29 vs West Bromwich Albion (a) 1-3
Att: 12,606 Galley

1973/74 SEASON
3rd Round
Jan 5 vs Bristol Rovers (h) 4-3
Att: 23,456 Martin 2, Chapman, Lyall (pen)
4th Round
Jan 27 vs Manchester C (h) 4-1
Att: 41,472 McKenzie, Bowyer 2, Lyall
5th Round
Feb 17 vs Portsmouth (h) 1-0
Att: 38,589 McKenzie (pen)
6th Round
Mar 9 vs Newcastle United (a) 3-4
Att: 54,000 Bowyer, O'Kane, Lyall
Match annulled due to crowd misbehaviour
Replay (at Goodison Park)
Mar 18 vs Newcastle United 0-0
Att: 40,685
2nd Replay (at Goodison Park)
Mar 21 vs Newcastle United 0-1
Att: 31,373

1974/75 SEASON
3rd Round
Jan 4 vs Tottenham Hotspur (h) 1-1
Att: 23,355 Jones
Replay
Jan 8 vs Tottenham Hotspur (a) 1-0
Att: 27,996 Martin

4th Round
Jan 28 vs Fulham (a) 0-0
Att: 20,000
Replay
Feb 3 vs Fulham (h) 1-1 (aet.)
Att: 25,361 Martin
2nd Replay
Feb 5 vs Fulham (a) 1-1 (aet.)
Att: 11,920 Slough
3rd Replay
Feb 10 vs Fulham (h) 1-2
Att: 23,240 Chapman

1975/76 SEASON
3rd Round
Jan 1 vs Peterborough United (h) 0-0
Att: 31,525
Replay
Jan 7 vs Peterborough United (a) 0-1
Att: 17,866

1976/77 SEASON
3rd Round
Jan 8 vs Bristol Rovers (h) 1-1
Att: 17,770 Robertson (pen)
Replay
Jan 11 vs Bristol Rovers (a) 1-1 (aet.)
Att: 12,348 Woodcock
2nd Replay (at Villa Park)
Jan 18 vs Bristol Rovers 6-0
Att: 5,736 Woodcock 2, Bowyer, Withe, Anderson, O'Hare
4th Round
Jan 29 vs Southampton (h) 3-3
Att: 38,204 Robertson 2 (1 pen), Woodcock
Replay
Feb 1 vs Southampton (a) 1-2
Att: 29,041 Woodcock

1977/78 SEASON
3rd Round
Jan 7 vs Swindon Town (h) 4-1
Att: 28,953 Woodcock 2, Withe, Robertson
4th Round
Jan 31 vs Manchester City (h) 2-1
Att: 38,509 Robertson, Withe
5th Round
Feb 18 vs Queen's Park Rangers (a) 1-1
Att: 26,803 O'Neill
Replay
Feb 27 vs Queen's Pk. Rangers (h) 1-1 (aet.)
Att: 40,097 Robertson (pen)
2nd Replay
Mar 2 vs Queen's Park Rangers (h) 3-1
Att: 32,000 O'Neill, Woodcock 2
6th Round
Mar 11 vs West Bromwich Albion (h) 0-2
Att: 38,000

1978/79 SEASON
3rd Round
Jan 10 vs Aston Villa (h) 2-0
Att: 29,550 Needham, Evans (og)
4th Round
Jan 27 vs York City (h) 3-1
Att: 25,228 Lloyd, McGovern, O'Neill
5th Round
Feb 26 vs Arsenal (h) 0-1
Att: 35,906

1979/80 SEASON
3rd Round
Jan 5 vs Leeds United (a) 4-1
Att: 35,945 Gray, Birtles, Bowyer, Robertson
4th Round
Jan 26 vs Liverpool (h) 0-2
Att: 33,277

1980/81 SEASON
3rd Round
Jan 3 vs Bolton Wanderers (h) 3-3
Att: 22,920 Francis 2, Ponte
Replay
Jan 6 vs Bolton Wanderers (a) 1-0 (aet.)
Att: 22,779 Francis
4th Round
Jan 24 vs Manchester United (h) 1-0
Att: 34,110 Francis
5th Round
Feb 14 vs Bristol City (h) 2-1
Att: 26,732 Robertson (pen), Wallace
6th Round
Mar 7 vs Ipswich Town (h) 3-3
Att: 34,796 Francis, Walsh, Robertson (pen)
Replay
Mar 10 vs Ipswich Town (a) 0-1
Att: 31,060

1981/82 SEASON
3rd Round
Jan 2 vs Wrexham (h) 1-3
Att: 15,649 Proctor

1982/83 SEASON
3rd Round
Jan 8 vs Derby County (a) 0-2
Att: 28,494

1983/84 SEASON
3rd Round
Jan 7 vs Southampton (h) 1-2
Att: 19,271 Hart

1984/85 SEASON
3rd Round
Jan 6 vs Newcastle United (h) 1-1
Att: 23,582 Bowyer
Replay
Jan 9 vs Newcastle Utd. (a) 3-1 (aet.)
(90 minutes 1-1)
Att: 25,166 Davenport (pen), Bowyer, Christie
4th Round
Jan 26 vs Wimbledon (h) 0-0
Att: 17,184
Replay
Jan 30 vs Wimbledon (a) 0-1
Att: 10,348

1985/86 SEASON
3rd Round
Jan 4 vs Blackburn Rovers (h) 1-1
Att: 15,772 Birtles
Replay
Jan 13 vs Blackburn Rovers (a) 2-3
Att: 11,710 Walsh, Birtles

1986/87 SEASON
3rd Round
Jan 11 vs Crystal Palace (a) 0-1
Att: 11,618

1987/88 SEASON
3rd Round
Jan 9 vs Halifax Town (a) 4-0
Att: 4,013 Wilson, Pearce, Plummer, Wilkinson
4th Round
Jan 30 vs Leyton Orient (a) 2-1
Att: 19,212 Glover, Plummer
5th Round
Feb 20 vs Birmingham City (a) 1-0
Att: 34,494 Crosby
6th Round
Mar 12 vs Arsenal (a) 2-1
Att: 50,157 Wilkinson, Rice

64

Semi-Final (at Hillsborough)
April 9 vs Liverpool 1-2
Att: 51,627 Clough

1988/89 SEASON
3rd Round
Jan 7 vs Ipswich Town (h) 3-0
Att: 20,743 Yallop (og), Gaynor, Chapman
4th Round
Jan 28 vs Leeds United (h) 2-0
Att: 28,107 Chapman, Parker
5th Round
Feb 19 vs Watford (a) 3-0
Att: 18,044 Webb, Chapman, Laws
6th Round
Mar 18 vs Manchester United (a) 1-0
Att: 55,052 Parker
Semi-Final (at Hillsborough)
Apr 15 vs Liverpool 0-0
Att: 53,000 Abandoned after 6 minutes
Replay
May 7 vs Liverpool (a) 1-3
Att: 38,000 Webb

1989/90 SEASON
3rd Round
Jan 7 vs Manchester United (h) 0-1
Att: 23,072

1990/91 SEASON
3rd Round
Jan 6 vs Crystal Palace (a) 0-0
Att: 15,396
Replay
Jan 21 vs Crystal Palace (h) 2-2 (aet.)
Att: 23,301 Wilson, Pearce
2nd Replay
Jan 28 vs Crystal Palace (h) 3-0
Att: 22,164 Parker 2, Crosby
4th Round
Feb 13 vs Newcastle United (a) 2-2
Att: 29,231 Pearce, Clough
Replay
Feb 18 vs Newcastle United (h) 3-0
Att: 28,962 Clough, Hodge, Parker
5th Round
Feb 25 vs Southampton (a) 1-1
Att: 18,512 Hodge
Replay
Mar 4 vs Southampton (h) 3-1
Att: 26,633 Jemson 3 (1 pen)
6th Round
Mar 9 vs Norwich City (a) 1-0
Att: 24,018 Keane
Semi-Final (at Villa Park)
Apr 14 vs West Ham United 4-0
Att: 40,041 Crosby, Keane, Pearce, Charles
FINAL (at Wembley)
May 18 vs Tottenham Hotspur 1-2 (aet.)
Att: 80,000 Pearce

1991/92 SEASON
3rd Round
Jan 4 vs Wolverhampton Wanderers (h) 1-0
Att: 27,068 Clough
4th Round
Jan 26 vs Hereford United (h) 2-0
Att: 24,259 Pearce, Sheringham
5th Round
Feb 15 vs Bristol City (h) 4-1
Att: 24,615 Llewellyn (og), Clough, Pearce, Sheringham (pen)
6th Round
Mar 7 vs Portsmouth (a) 0-1
Att: 25,402

1992/93 SEASON
3rd Round
Jan 3 vs Southampton (h) 2-1
Att: 13,592 Keane, Webb
4th Round
Jan 23 vs Middlesbrough (h) 1-1
Att: 22,296 Webb
Replay
Feb 3 vs Middlesbrough (a) 3-0
Att: 20,514 Bannister, Clough, Woan
5th Round
Feb 13 vs Arsenal (a) 0-2
Att: 27,591

1993/94 SEASON
3rd Round
Jan 8 vs Sheffield Wednesday (a) 1-1
Att: 32,488 Cooper
Replay
Jan 19 vs Sheffield Wednesday (h) 0-2
Att: 25,268

1994/95 SEASON
3rd Round
Jan 7 vs Plymouth Argyle (h) 2-0
Att: 19,821 Collymore, Gemmill
4th Round
Jan 28 vs Crystal Palace (h) 1-2
Att: 16,790 Bohinen

LEAGUE CUP COMPETITION

1969/70 SEASON
2nd Round
Sep 3 vs Barrow (a) 2-1
Att: 8,919 Barnwell, Moore
3rd Round
Sep 23 vs West Ham United (h) 1-0
Att: 20,929 Lyons
4th Round
Oct 14 vs Oxford United (h) 0-1
Att: 20,734

1970/71 SEASON
2nd Round
Sep 9 vs Huddersfield Town (a) 0-0
Att: 18,165
Replay
Sep 19 vs Huddersfield Town (h) 2-0
Att: 15,818 Cormack, Moore
3rd Round
Oct 6 vs Birmingham City (a) 1-2
Att: 23,015 Hockey (og)

1971/72 SEASON
2nd Round
Sep 7 vs Aldershot (h) 5-1
Att: 8,380 McKenzie 2, Martin, Fraser, Cormack
3rd Round
Oct 6 vs Chelsea (h) 1-1
Att: 16,811 McKenzie
Replay
Oct 11 vs Chelsea (a) 1-2
Att: 24,817 Moore

1972/73 SEASON
2nd Round
Sep 5 vs Aston Villa (h) 0-1
Att: 17,665

1973/74 SEASON
2nd Round
Oct 10 vs Millwall (a) 0-0
Att: 8,631
Replay
Oct 16 vs Millwall (h) 1-3
Att: 9,241

1974/75 SEASON
2nd Round
Sep 10 vs Newcastle United (h) 1-1
Att: 14,183 Bowyer
Replay
Sep 25 vs Newcastle United (a) 0-3
Att: 26,226

1975/76 SEASON
1st Round (1st leg)
Aug 19 vs Rotherham United (a) 2-1
Att: 4,912 Chapman, McGovern
1st Round (2nd leg)
Aug 27 vs Rotherham Utd. (h) 5-1 (agg. 7-2)
Att: 7,977 Lyall 2 pens, Richardson 2, Bowyer
2nd Round
Sep 10 vs Plymouth Argyle (h) 1-0
Att: 8,978 Bowyer
3rd Round
Oct 8 vs Manchester City (a) 1-2
Att: 26,536 Bowyer

1976/77 SEASON
2nd Round
Aug 31 vs Walsall (a) 4-2
Att: 8,437 Curran, Barrett, O'Neill 2
3rd Round
Sep 21 vs Coventry City (h) 0-3
Att: 15,969

1977/78 SEASON
2nd Round
Aug 30 vs West Ham United (h) 5-0
Att: 18,224 O'Neill, Bowyer 2, Woodcock, Withe
3rd Round
Oct 25 vs Notts County (h) 4-0
Att: 26,931 Robertson (pen), Woodcock, Bowyer 2
4th Round
Nov 29 vs Aston Villa (h) 4-2
Att: 29,333 Lloyd, Anderson, Withe, Woodcock
5th Round
Jan 17 vs Bury (a) 3-0
Att: 21,500 Bowyer, O'Neill, Robertson
Semi-Final (1st leg)
Feb 8 vs Leeds United (a) 3-1
Att: 43,222 Withe 2, O'Hare
Semi-Final (2nd leg)
Feb 22 vs Leeds United (h) 4-2 (agg. 7-3)
Att: 38,131 Withe, Bowyer, O'Neill, Woodcock
FINAL
Mar 18 vs Liverpool 0-0 (aet.)
Att: 100,000 (at Wembley)
Replay
Mar 22 vs Liverpool 1-0
Att: 54,375 (at Old Trafford) Robertson (pen)

1978/79 SEASON
2nd Round
Aug 29 vs Oldham Athletic (a) 0-0
Att: 13,793
Replay
Sep 6 vs Oldham Atheltic (h) 4-2
Att: 18,669 Needham, Burns, Woodcock, Robertson (pen)
3rd Round
Oct 4 vs Oxford United (a) 5-0
Att: 14,287 Birtles, McGovern, O'Neill, Robertson, Anderson
4th Round
Nov 7 vs Everton (a) 3-2
Att: 48,503 Lloyd, Anderson, Woodcock

5th Round
Dec 13 vs Brighton & Hove Albion (h) 3-1
Att: 30,672 McGovern, Robertson, Birtles
Semi-Final (1st leg)
Jan 17 vs Watford (h) 3-1
Att: 32,538 Birtles 2, Robertson
Semi-Final (2nd leg)
Jan 30 vs Watford (a) 0-0 (aggregate 3-1)
Att: 27,656
FINAL
Mar 17 vs Southampton 3-2
Att: 100,000 (at Wembley) Birtles 2, Woodcock

1979/80 SEASON
2nd Round (1st leg)
Aug 29 vs Blackburn Rovers (a) 1-1
Att: 20,458 Gray
2nd Round (2nd leg)
Sep 15 vs Blackburn Rovers (h) 6-1 (agg. 7-2)
Att: 21,244 Gray, Woodcock, Bowyer 2, Robertson 2 (1 pen)
3rd Round
Sep 25 vs Middlesbrough (a) 3-1
Att: 29,064 Woodcock 3
4th Round
Oct 30 vs Bristol City (a) 1-1
Att: 25,695 O'Hare
Replay
Nov 14 vs Bristol City (h) 3-0
Att: 20,462 O'Neill, Anderson, Woodcock
5th Round
Dec 4 vs West Ham United (a) 0-0
Att: 35,386
Replay
Dec 12 vs West Ham United (h) 3-0 (aet.)
Att: 25,462 O'Hare, Birtles, O'Neill
Semi-Final (1st leg)
Jan 22 vs Liverpool (h) 1-0
Att: 32,234 Robertson (pen)
Semi-Final (2nd leg)
Feb 12 vs Liverpool (a) 1-1 (aggregate 2-1)
Att: 50,880 Robertson (pen)
FINAL
Mar 15 vs Wolverhampton Wanderers 0-1
Att: 100,000 (at Wembley)

1980/81 SEASON
2nd Round (1st leg)
Aug 27 vs Peterborough United (h) 3-0
Att: 16,117 Robertson (pen), Birtles, Gray
2nd Round (2nd leg)
Sep 3 vs Peterborough United (a) 1-1 (agg. 4-1)
Att: 11,503 Mills
3rd Round
Sep 23 vs Bury (a) 7-0
Att: 8,828 Ponte 3, Mills, Anderson, Birtles 2
4th Round
Oct 28 vs Watford (a) 1-4
Att: 22,597 Wallace

1981/82 SEASON
2nd Round (1st leg)
Oct 6 vs Birmingham City (a) 3-2
Att: 14,330 Wallace 2, Proctor
2nd Round (2nd leg)
Oct 28 vs Birmingham City (h) 2-1 (agg. 5-3)
Att: 16,316 Needham, Robertson
3rd Round
Nov 11 vs Blackburn Rovers (a) 1-0
Att: 14,752 Fashanu

4th Round
Dec 2 vs Tranmere Rovers (h) 2-0
Att: 12,244 Wallace, Rober
5th Round
Jan 18 vs Tottenham Hotspur (a) 0-1
Att: 31,192

1982/83 SEASON
2nd Round (1st leg)
Oct 6 vs West Bromwich Albion (h) 6-1
Att: 11,969 Wallace 2, Robertson 2 pens, Hodge, Birtles
2nd Round (2nd leg)
Oct 27 vs West Brom. Alb. (a) 1-3 (agg. 7-4)
Att: 6,536 Birtles
3rd Round
Nov 10 vs Watford (h) 7-3
Att: 14,873 Young, Proctor 2, Birtles 2, Bowyer, Wallace
4th Round
Dec 1 vs Brentford (h) 2-0
Att: 16,479 Wallace, Robertson (pen)
5th Round
Jan 19 vs Manchester United (a) 0-4
Att: 44,400

1983/84 SEASON
2nd Round (1st leg)
Oct 4 vs Wimbledon (a) 0-2
Att: 7,554
2nd Round (2nd leg)
Oct 26 vs Wimbledon (h) 1-1 (agg. 1-3)
Att: 13,718 Wallace

1984/85 SEASON
2nd Round (1st leg)
Sep 25 vs Portsmouth (a) 0-1
Att: 20,409
2nd Round (2nd leg)
Oct 10 vs Portsmouth (h) 3-0 (aet) (agg 3-1)
Att: 18,128 Hodge, Wigley, Gunn
3rd Round
Oct 31 vs Sunderland (h) 1-1
Att: 14,291 Christie
Replay
Nov 6 vs Sunderland (a) 0-1 (aet.)
(90 minutes 0-0)
Att: 23,184

1985/86 SEASON
2nd Round (1st leg)
Sep 25 vs Bolton Wanderers (h) 4-0
Att: 10,530 Campbell 2, Rice, Clough
2nd Round (2nd leg)
Oct 7 vs Bolton Wands. (a) 3-0 (agg. 7-0)
Att: 4,010 Rice, Davenport, Clough
3rd Round
Oct 30 vs Derby County (a) 2-1
Att: 25,000 Metgod, Carr
4th Round
Nov 25 vs Queen's Park Rangers (a) 1-3
Att: 13,052 Clough

1986/87 SEASON
2nd Round (1st leg)
Sep 24 vs Brighton & Hove Albion (a) 0-0
Att: 13,266
2nd Round (2nd leg)
Oct 8 vs Brighton & H. A. (h) 3-0 (agg. 3-0)
Att: 16,036 Carr 2, Pearce
3rd Round
Oct 29 vs Crystal Palace (a) 2-2
Att: 12,020 Pearce (pen), Birtles
Replay
Nov 5 vs Crystal Palace (h) 1-0
Att: 13,029 Clough

4th Round
Nov 19 vs Bradford City (a) 5-0
Att: 16,009 Carr, Metgod, Clough, Mills, Fairclough
5th Round
Jan 21 vs Arsenal (a) 0-2
Att: 38,617

1987/88 SEASON
2nd Round (1st leg)
Sep 23 vs Hereford United (h) 5-0
Att: 11,617 Webb 2, Carr, Clough, Wilkinson
2nd Round (2nd leg)
Oct 7 vs Hereford United (a) 1-1 (agg. 6-1)
Att: 3,905 Clough
3rd Round
Oct 27 vs Manchester City (a) 0-3
Att: 15,168

1988/89 SEASON
2nd Round (1st leg)
Sep 28 vs Chester City (h) 6-0
Att: 11,958 Pearce, Clough 2, Webb, Hodge, Gaynor
2nd Round (2nd leg)
Oct 12 vs Chester City (a) 4-0 (agg. 10-0)
Att: 4,747 Gaynor 3, Crosby
3rd Round
Nov 2 vs Coventry City (h) 3-2
Att: 21,201 Foster, Hodge, Clough
4th Round
Nov 30 vs Leicester City (a) 0-0
Att: 26,704
Replay
Dec 14 vs Leicester City (h) 2-1
Att: 26,676 Clough, Chapman
5th Round
Jan 18 vs Queen's Park Rangers (h) 5-2
Att: 24,065 Chapman 4, Clough (pen)
Semi-Final (1st leg)
Feb 15 vs Bristol City (h) 1-1
Att: 28,084 Pender (og)
Semi-Final (2nd leg)
Feb 26 vs Bristol C. (a) 1-0 (aet) (agg. 2-1)
Att: 28,084 Parker
FINAL
Apr 9 vs Luton Town 3-1
Att: 76,130 (at Wembley) Clough 2 (1 pen), Webb

1989/90 SEASON
2nd Round (1st leg)
Sep 20 vs Huddersfield Town (h) 1-1
Att: 18,976 Crosby
2nd Round (2nd leg)
Oct 3 vs Hudd'field T. (a) 3-3 (aet) (agg 4-4)
Att: 13,262 Gaynor, Crosby, Clough
Nottingham Forest won on Away Goals
3rd Round
Oct 24 vs Crystal Palace (a) 0-0
Att: 14,250
Replay
Nov 1 vs Crystal Palace (h) 5-0
Att: 18,625 Hodge 2, Clough, Pearce, Hopkins (og)
4th Round
Nov 22 vs Everton (h) 1-0
Att: 21,324 Chapman
5th Round
Jan 17 vs Tottenham Hotspur (h) 2-2
Att: 30,044 Crosby, Parker
Replay
Jan 24 vs Tottenham Hotspur (a) 3-2
Att: 32,357 Hodge 2, Jemson

Semi-Final (1st leg)
Feb 11 vs Coventry City (h) 2-1
Att: 26,153 Clough (pen), Pearce
Semi-Final (2nd leg)
Feb 25 vs Coventry City (a) 0-0 (agg. 2-1)
Att: 25,900
FINAL
Apr 29 vs Oldham Athletic 1-0
Att: 74,343 (at Wembley) Jemson

1990/91 SEASON
2nd Round (1st leg)
Sep 26 vs Burnley (h) 4-1
Att: 17,987 Chettle, Keane, Jemson, Pearce
2nd Round (2nd leg)
Oct 10 vs Burnley (a) 1-0 (aggregate 5-1)
Att: 11,399 Crosby
3rd Round
Oct 31 vs Plymouth Argyle (a) 2-1
Att: 17,467 Parker, Jemson
4th Round
Nov 28 vs Coventry City (a) 4-5
Att: 16,304 Clough 3, Parker

1991/92 SEASON
2nd Round (1st leg)
Sep 25 vs Bolton Wanderers (h) 4-0
Att: 19,936 Keane, Gaynor 2, Black
2nd Round (2nd leg)
Oct 8 vs Bolton Wanderers (a) 5-2 (agg. 9-2)
Att: 5,469 Sheringham, Keane 2, Gaynor, Black
3rd Round
Oct 30 vs Bristol Rovers (h) 2-0
Att: 17,529 Glover, Gemmill
4th Round
Dec 4 vs Southampton (h) 0-0
Att: 17,939
Replay
Dec 17 vs Southampton (a) 1-0
Att: 10,861 Gemmill
5th Round
Jan 8 vs Crystal Palace (a) 1-1
Att: 14,941 Clough
Replay
Feb 5 vs Crystal Palace (h) 4-2
Att: 18,918 Sheringham 3, Pearce
Semi-Final (1st leg)
Feb 9 vs Tottenham Hotspur (h) 1-1
Att: 21,402 Sheringham
Semi-Final (2nd leg)
Mar 1 vs Tott. Hotspur (a) 2-1 (aet) (agg 3-2)
Att: 28,216 Glover, Keane
FINAL
Apr 12 vs Manchester United 0-1
Att: 76,810 (at Wembley)

1992/93 SEASON
2nd Round (1st leg)
Sep 23 vs Stockport County (a) 3-2
Att: 7,964 Bannister, Clough, Orlygsson
2nd Round (2nd leg)
Oct 7 vs Stockport County (h) 2-1 (agg. 5-3)
Att: 15,573 Black, Gannon (og)
3rd Round
Oct 28 vs Crewe Alexandra (a) 1-0
Att: 7,042 Orlygsson
4th Round
Dec 2 vs Tottenham Hostpur (h) 2-0
Att: 22,312 Woan, Keane
5th Round
Jan 12 vs Arsenal (a) 0-2
Att: 25,600

1993/94 SEASON
2nd Round (1st leg)
Sep 21 vs Wrexham (a) 3-3
Att: 7,860 Collymore 3
2nd Round (2nd leg)
Oct 6 vs Wrexham (h) 3-1 (aggregate 6-4)
Att: 11,619 Black, Crosby, Collymore
3rd Round
Oct 27 vs West Ham United (h) 2-1
Att: 17,857 Black, Collymore
4th Round
Dec 1 vs Manchester City (h) 0-0
Att: 22,195
Replay
Dec 15 vs Manchester City (a) 2-1
Att: 14,117 Webb, Cooper
5th Round
Jan 26 vs Tranmere Rovers (h) 1-1
Att: 20,066 Gemmill
Replay
Jan 29 vs Tranmere Rovers (a) 0-2
Att: 12,578

1994/95 SEASON
2nd Round (1st leg)
Sep 21 vs Hereford United (h) 2-1
Att: 10,076 Collymore 2
2nd Round (2nd leg)
Oct 4 Hereford United (a) 0-0 (agg. 2-1)
Att: 8,953
3rd Round
Oct 26 vs Wolverhampton Wanderers (a) 3-2
Att: 28,369 Pearce, Roy 2
4th Round
Nov 30 vs Millwall (h) 0-2
Att: 12,393

EUROPEAN CUP
1978/79 SEASON
1st Round (1st leg)
Sep 13 vs Liverpool (h) 2-0
Att: 38,316 Birtles, Barrett
1st Round (2nd leg)
Sep 27 vs Liverpool (a) 0-0 (aggregate 2-0)
Att: 51,679
2nd Round (1st leg)
Oct 18 vs AEK Athens (a) 2-1
Att: 35,000 McGovern, Birtles
2nd Round (2nd leg)
Nov 1st vs AEK Athens (h) 5-1 (agg. 7-2)
Att: 38,069 Needham, Woodcock, Anderson, Birtles 2
Quarter-Final (1st leg)
Mar 7 vs Grasshopper Zürich (h) 4-1
Att: 31,949 Birtles, Robertson (pen), Gemmill, Lloyd
Quarter-Final (2nd leg)
Mar 21 vs G'hopper Zürich (a) 1-1 (agg. 5-2)
Att: 17,800 O'Neill
Semi-Final (1st leg)
Apr 11 vs 1.FC Cologne (h) 3-3
Att: 40,804 Birtles, Bowyer, Robertson
Semi-Final (2nd leg)
Apr 25 vs 1.FC Cologne (a) 1-0 (agg. 4-3)
Att: 60,000 Bowyer
FINAL (in Munich)
May 30 vs Malmö FF 1-0
Att: 57,000 Francis

1979/80 SEASON
1st Round (1st leg)
Sep 19 vs Östers IF (h) 2-0
Att: 21,971 Bowyer, Hallan (og)

1st Round (2nd leg)
Oct 3 vs Östers IF (a) 1-1 (aggregate 3-1)
Att: 14,772 Woodcock
2nd Round (1st leg)
Oct 24 vs FC Arges Pitesti (h) 2-0
Att: 24,828 Woodcock, Birtles
2nd Round (2nd leg)
Nov 7 vs FC Arges Pitesti (a) 2-1 (agg. 4-1)
Att: 22,000 Bowyer, Birtles
Quarter-Final (1st leg)
Mar 5 vs Dynamo Berlin (h) 0-1
Att: 27,946
Quarter-Final (2nd leg)
Mar 18 vs Dynamo Berlin (a) 3-1 (agg. 3-2)
Att: 27,000 Francis 2, Robertson (pen)
Semi-Final (1st leg)
Apr 9 vs Ajax (h) 2-0
Att: 31,244 Francis, Robertson (pen)
Semi-Final (2nd leg)
Apr 23 vs Ajax (a) 0-1 (aggregate 2-1)
Att: 60,000
FINAL (in Madrid)
May 28 vs Hamburger SV 1-0
Att: 50,000 Robertson

1980/81 SEASON
1st Round (1st leg)
Sep 17 vs CFKA Sredets (a) 0-1
Att: 70,000
1st Round (2nd leg)
Oct 1 vs CFKA Sredets (h) 0-1 (agg. 0-2)
Att: 25,818

UEFA CUP COMPETITION
1983/84 SEASON
1st Round (1st leg)
Sep 14 vs FC Vorwärts Frankfurt (h) 2-0
Att: 14,994 (at Oder) Wallace, Hodge
1st Round (2nd leg)
Sep 28 vs FC Vor. Frankfurt (a) 1-0 (agg 3-0)
Att: 18,000 Bowyer
2nd Round (1st leg)
Oct 19 vs PSV Eindhoven (a) 2-1
Att: 28,000 Davenport, Walsh (pen)
2nd Round (2nd leg)
Nov 2 vs PSV Eindhoven (h) 1-0 (agg. 3-1)
Att: 16,943 Davenport
3rd Round (1st leg)
Nov 23 vs Celtic (h) 0-0
Att: 32,017
3rd Round (2nd leg)
Dev 7 vs Celtic (a) 2-1 (aggregate 2-1)
Att: 66,938 Hodge, Walsh
Quarter-Final (1st leg)
Mar 7 vs SK Sturm Graz (h) 1-0
Att: 19,459 Hart
Quarter-Final (2nd leg)
Mar 21 vs SK Sturm Graz (a) 1-1 (agg. 2-1)
Att: 21,000 Walsh (pen)
Semi-Final (1st leg)
Apr 11 vs Anderlecht (h) 2-0
Att: 22,681 Hodge 2
Semi-Final (2nd leg)
Apr 25 vs Anderlecht (a) 0-3 (agg. 2-3)
Att: 36,000

1984/85 SEASON
1st Round (1st leg)
Sep 19 vs Club Brugge KV (h) 0-0
Att: 18,307
1st Round (2nd leg)
Oct 3 vs Club Brugge KV (a) 0-1 (agg. 0-1)
Att: 20,000

1970-71 SEASON

FIRST DIVISION

Arsenal	42	29	7	6	71	29	65
Leeds United	42	27	10	5	72	30	64
Tottenham Hotspur	42	19	14	9	54	33	52
Wolves	42	22	8	12	64	54	52
Liverpool	42	17	17	8	42	24	51
Chelsea	42	18	15	9	52	42	51
Southampton	42	17	12	13	56	44	46
Manchester United	42	16	11	15	65	66	43
Derby County	42	16	10	16	56	54	42
Coventry City	42	16	10	16	37	38	42
Manchester City	42	12	17	13	47	42	41
Newcastle United	42	14	13	15	44	46	41
Stoke City	42	12	13	17	44	48	37
Everton	42	12	13	17	54	60	37
Huddersfield Town	42	11	14	17	40	49	36
Nottingham Forest	**42**	**14**	**8**	**20**	**42**	**61**	**36**
West Brom. Albion	42	10	15	17	58	75	35
Crystal Palace	42	12	11	19	39	57	35
Ipswich Town	42	12	10	20	42	48	34
West Ham United	42	10	14	18	47	60	34
Burnley	42	7	13	22	29	63	27
Blackpool	42	4	15	23	34	66	23

1971-72 SEASON

FIRST DIVISION

Derby County	42	24	10	8	69	33	58
Leeds United	42	24	9	9	73	31	57
Liverpool	42	24	9	9	64	30	57
Manchester City	42	23	11	8	77	45	57
Arsenal	42	22	8	12	58	40	52
Tottenham Hotspur	42	19	13	10	63	42	51
Chelsea	42	18	12	12	58	49	48
Manchester United	42	19	10	13	69	61	48
Wolves	42	18	11	13	65	57	47
Sheffield United	42	17	12	13	61	60	46
Newcastle United	42	15	11	16	49	52	41
Leicester City	42	13	13	16	41	46	39
Ipswich Town	42	11	16	15	39	53	38
West Ham United	42	12	12	18	47	51	36
Everton	42	9	18	15	37	48	36
West Brom. Albion	42	12	11	19	42	54	35
Stoke City	42	10	15	17	39	56	35
Coventry City	42	9	15	18	44	67	33
Southampton	42	12	7	23	52	80	31
Crystal Palace	42	8	13	21	39	65	29
Nottingham Forest	**42**	**8**	**9**	**25**	**47**	**81**	**25**
Huddersfield Town	42	6	13	23	27	59	25

1972-73 SEASON

SECOND DIVISION

Burnley	42	24	14	4	72	35	62
Q.P.R.	42	24	13	5	81	37	61
Aston Villa	42	18	14	10	51	47	50
Middlesbrough	42	17	13	12	46	43	47
Bristol City	42	17	12	13	63	51	46
Sunderland	42	17	12	13	59	49	46
Blackpool	42	18	10	14	56	51	46
Oxford United	42	19	7	16	52	43	45
Fulham	42	16	12	14	58	49	44
Sheffield Wednesday	42	17	10	15	59	55	44
Millwall	42	16	10	16	55	47	42
Luton Town	42	15	11	16	44	43	41
Hull City	42	14	12	16	64	49	40
Nottingham Forest	**42**	**14**	**12**	**16**	**47**	**52**	**40**
Orient	42	12	12	18	49	53	36
Swindon Town	42	10	16	16	46	60	36
Portsmouth	42	12	11	19	42	59	35
Carlisle United	42	11	12	19	50	52	34
Preston North End	42	11	12	19	37	64	34
Cardiff City	42	11	11	20	43	58	33
Huddersfield Town	42	8	17	17	36	56	33
Brighton & Hove Alb.	42	8	13	21	46	83	29

1973-74 SEASON

SECOND DIVISION

Middlesbrough	42	27	11	4	77	30	65
Luton Town	42	19	12	11	64	51	50
Carlisle United	42	20	9	13	61	48	49
Orient	42	15	18	9	55	42	48
Blackpool	42	17	13	12	57	40	47
Sunderland	42	19	9	14	58	44	47
Nottingham Forest	**42**	**15**	**15**	**12**	**57**	**43**	**45**
West Brom. Albion	42	14	16	12	48	45	44
Hull City	42	13	17	12	46	47	43
Notts County	42	15	13	14	55	60	43
Bolton Wanderers	42	15	12	15	44	40	42
Millwall	42	14	14	14	51	51	42
Fulham	42	16	10	16	39	43	42
Aston Villa	42	13	15	14	48	45	41
Portsmouth	42	14	12	16	45	62	40
Bristol City	42	14	10	18	47	54	38
Cardiff City	42	10	16	16	49	62	36
Oxford United	42	10	16	16	35	46	36
Sheffield Wednesday	42	12	11	19	51	63	35
Crystal Palace	42	11	12	19	43	56	34
Preston North End *	42	9	14	19	40	62	31
Swindon Town	42	7	11	24	36	72	25

* Preston - one point deducted for fielding ineligible player

1974-75 SEASON

SECOND DIVISION

Manchester United	42	26	9	7	66	30	61
Aston Villa	42	25	8	9	69	32	58
Norwich City	42	20	13	9	58	37	53
Sunderland	42	19	13	10	65	35	51
Bristol City	42	21	8	13	47	33	50
West Brom. Albion	42	18	9	15	54	42	45
Blackpool	42	14	17	11	38	33	45
Hull City	42	15	14	13	40	53	44
Fulham	42	13	16	13	44	39	42
Bolton	42	15	12	15	45	41	42
Oxford United	42	15	12	15	41	51	42
Orient	42	11	20	11	28	39	42
Southampton	42	15	11	16	53	54	41
Notts County	42	12	16	14	49	59	40
York City	42	14	10	18	51	55	38
Nottingham Forest	**42**	**12**	**14**	**16**	**43**	**55**	**38**
Portsmouth	42	12	13	17	44	54	37
Oldham Athletic	42	10	15	17	40	48	35
Bristol Rovers	42	12	11	19	42	64	35
Millwall	42	10	12	20	44	56	32
Cardiff City	42	9	14	19	36	62	32
Sheffield Wednesday	42	5	11	26	29	64	21

1975-76 SEASON

SECOND DIVISION

Sunderland	42	24	8	10	67	36	56
Bristol City	42	19	15	8	59	35	53
West Brom. Albion	42	20	13	9	50	33	53
Bolton Wanderers	42	20	12	10	64	38	52
Notts County	42	19	11	12	60	41	49
Southampton	42	21	7	14	66	50	49
Luton Town	42	19	10	13	61	51	48
Nottingham Forest	**42**	**17**	**12**	**13**	**55**	**40**	**46**
Charlton Athletic	42	15	12	15	61	72	42
Blackpool	42	14	14	14	40	49	42
Chelsea	42	12	16	14	53	54	40
Fulham	42	13	14	15	45	47	40
Orient	42	13	14	15	37	39	40
Hull City	42	14	11	17	45	49	39
Blackburn Rovers	42	12	14	16	45	50	38
Plymouth Argyle	42	13	12	17	48	54	38
Oldham Athletic	42	13	12	17	57	68	38
Bristol Rovers	42	11	16	15	38	50	38
Carlisle United	42	12	13	17	45	59	37
Oxford United	42	11	11	20	39	59	33
York City	42	10	8	24	39	71	28
Portsmouth	42	9	7	26	32	61	25

1976-77 SEASON

SECOND DIVISION

Wolves	42	22	13	7	84	45	57
Chelsea	42	21	13	8	73	53	55
Nottingham Forest	**42**	**21**	**10**	**11**	**77**	**43**	**52**
Bolton Wanderers	42	20	11	11	74	54	51
Blackpool	42	17	17	8	58	42	51
Luton Town	42	23	6	15	67	48	48
Charlton Athletic	42	16	16	10	71	58	48
Notts County	42	19	10	13	65	60	48
Southampton	42	17	10	15	72	67	44
Millwall	42	17	13	14	57	53	43
Sheffield United	42	14	12	16	54	63	40
Blackburn Rovers	42	15	9	18	42	54	39
Oldham Athletic	42	14	10	18	52	64	38
Hull City	42	10	17	15	45	53	37
Bristol Rovers	42	12	13	17	53	68	37
Burnley	42	11	14	17	46	64	36
Fulham	42	11	13	18	44	61	35
Cardiff City	42	12	10	20	56	67	34
Orient	42	9	16	17	37	55	34
Carlisle United	42	11	12	19	49	75	34
Plymouth Argyle	42	8	16	18	46	65	32
Hereford United	42	8	15	19	57	78	31

1977-78 SEASON

FIRST DIVISION

Nottingham Forest	**42**	**25**	**14**	**3**	**69**	**24**	**64**
Liverpool	42	24	9	9	65	34	57
Everton	42	22	11	9	76	45	55
Manchester City	42	20	12	10	74	51	52
Arsenal	42	21	10	11	60	37	52
West Brom. Albion	42	18	14	10	62	53	50
Coventry City	42	18	12	12	75	62	48
Aston Villa	42	18	10	14	57	42	46
Leeds United	42	18	10	14	63	53	46
Manchester United	42	16	10	16	67	63	42
Birmingham City	42	16	9	17	55	60	41
Derby County	42	14	13	15	54	59	41
Norwich City	42	11	18	13	52	66	40
Middlesbrough	42	12	15	15	42	54	39
Wolves	42	12	12	18	51	64	36
Chelsea	42	11	14	17	46	69	36
Bristol City	42	11	13	18	49	53	35
Ipswich Town	42	11	13	18	47	61	35
Q.P.R.	42	9	15	18	47	64	33
West Ham United	42	12	8	22	52	69	32
Newcastle United	42	6	10	26	42	78	22
Leicester City	42	5	12	25	26	70	22

1978-79 SEASON

FIRST DIVISION

Liverpool	42	30	8	4	85	16	68
Nottingham Forest	**42**	**21**	**18**	**3**	**61**	**26**	**60**
West Brom. Albion	42	24	11	7	72	35	59
Everton	42	17	17	8	52	40	51
Leeds United	42	18	14	10	70	52	50
Ipswich Town	42	20	9	13	63	49	49
Arsenal	42	17	14	11	61	48	48
Aston Villa	42	15	16	11	59	49	46
Manchester United	42	15	15	12	60	63	45
Coventry City	42	14	16	12	58	68	44
Tottenham Hotspur	42	13	15	14	48	61	41
Middlesbrough	42	15	10	17	57	50	40
Bristol City	42	15	10	17	47	51	40
Southampton	42	12	16	14	47	53	40
Manchester City	42	13	13	16	58	56	39
Norwich City	42	7	23	12	51	57	37
Bolton Wanderers	42	12	11	19	54	75	35
Wolves	42	13	8	21	44	68	34
Derby County	42	10	11	21	44	71	31
Q.P.R.	42	6	13	23	45	73	25
Birmingham City	42	6	10	26	37	64	22
Chelsea	42	5	10	27	44	92	20

1979-80 SEASON

FIRST DIVISION

Liverpool	42	25	10	7	81	30	60
Manchester United	42	24	10	8	65	35	58
Ipswich Town	42	22	9	11	68	39	53
Arsenal	42	18	16	8	52	36	52
Nottingham Forest	**42**	**20**	**8**	**14**	**63**	**43**	**48**
Wolves	42	19	9	14	58	47	47
Aston Villa	42	16	14	12	51	50	46
Southampton	42	18	9	15	65	53	45
Middlesbrough	42	16	12	14	50	44	44
West Brom. Albion	42	11	19	12	54	50	41
Leeds United	42	13	14	15	46	50	40
Norwich City	42	13	14	15	58	66	40
Crystal Palace	42	12	16	14	41	50	40
Tottenham Hotspur	42	15	10	17	52	62	40
Coventry City	42	16	7	19	56	66	39
Brighton & Hove Alb.	42	11	15	16	47	57	37
Manchester City	42	12	13	17	43	66	37
Stoke City	42	13	10	19	44	58	36
Everton	42	9	17	16	43	51	35
Bristol City	42	9	13	20	37	66	31
Derby County	42	11	8	23	47	67	30
Bolton Wanderers	42	5	15	22	38	73	25

1980-81 SEASON

FIRST DIVISION

Aston Villa	42	26	8	8	72	40	60
Ipswich Town	42	23	10	9	77	43	56
Arsenal	42	19	15	8	61	45	53
West Brom. Albion	42	20	12	10	60	42	52
Liverpool	42	17	17	8	62	46	51
Southampton	42	20	10	12	76	56	50
Nottingham Forest	**42**	**19**	**12**	**11**	**62**	**45**	**50**
Manchester United	42	15	18	9	51	36	48
Leeds United	42	17	10	15	39	47	44
Tottenham Hotspur	42	14	15	13	70	68	43
Stoke City	42	12	18	12	51	60	42
Manchester City	42	14	11	17	56	59	39
Birmingham City	42	13	12	17	50	61	38
Middlesbrough	42	16	5	21	53	51	37
Everton	42	13	10	19	55	58	36
Coventry City	42	13	10	19	48	68	36
Sunderland	42	14	7	21	58	53	35
Wolves	42	13	9	20	47	55	35
Brighton & Hove Alb.	42	14	7	21	54	67	35
Norwich City	42	13	7	22	49	73	33
Leicester City	42	13	6	23	40	67	32
Crystal Palace	42	6	7	29	47	83	19

1981-82 SEASON

FIRST DIVISION

Liverpool	42	26	9	7	80	32	87
Ipswich Town	42	26	5	11	75	53	83
Manchester United	42	22	12	8	59	29	78
Tottenham Hotspur	42	20	11	11	67	48	71
Arsenal	42	20	11	11	48	37	71
Swansea City	42	21	6	15	58	51	69
Southampton	42	19	9	14	72	67	66
Everton	42	17	13	12	56	50	64
West Ham United	42	14	16	12	66	57	58
Manchester City	42	15	13	14	49	50	58
Aston Villa	42	15	12	15	55	53	57
Nottingham Forest	**42**	**15**	**12**	**15**	**42**	**48**	**57**
Brighton & Hove Alb.	42	13	13	16	43	52	52
Coventry City	42	13	11	18	56	62	50
Notts County	42	13	8	21	45	69	47
Birmingham City	42	10	14	18	53	61	44
West Brom. Albion	42	11	11	20	46	57	44
Stoke City	42	12	8	22	44	63	44
Sunderland	42	11	11	20	38	58	44
Leeds United	42	10	12	20	39	61	42
Wolves	42	10	10	22	32	63	40
Middlesbrough	42	8	15	19	34	52	39

1982-83 SEASON

FIRST DIVISION

Liverpool	42	24	10	8	87	37	82
Watford	42	22	5	15	74	57	71
Manchester United	42	19	13	8	56	38	70
Tottenham Hotspur	42	20	9	13	65	50	69
Nottingham Forest	**42**	**20**	**9**	**13**	**62**	**50**	**69**
Aston Villa	42	21	5	16	62	50	68
Everton	42	18	10	14	66	48	64
West Ham United	42	20	4	18	68	62	64
Ipswich Town	42	15	13	14	64	50	58
Arsenal	42	16	10	16	58	56	58
West Brom. Albion	42	15	12	15	51	49	57
Southampton	42	15	12	15	54	58	57
Stoke City	42	16	9	17	53	64	57
Norwich City	42	14	12	16	52	58	54
Notts County	42	15	7	21	55	71	52
Sunderland	42	12	14	16	48	61	50
Birmingham City	42	12	15	16	40	55	50
Luton Town	42	12	13	17	65	84	49
Coventry City	42	13	9	20	48	59	48
Manchester City	42	13	8	21	47	70	47
Swansea City	42	10	11	21	51	69	41
Brighton & Hove Alb.	42	9	13	20	38	67	40

1983-84 SEASON

FIRST DIVISION

Liverpool	42	22	14	6	73	32	80
Southampton	42	22	11	9	66	38	77
Nottingham Forest	**42**	**22**	**8**	**12**	**76**	**45**	**74**
Manchester United	42	20	14	8	71	41	74
Q.P.R.	42	22	7	13	67	37	73
Arsenal	42	19	9	15	74	60	63
Everton	42	16	14	12	44	42	62
Tottenham Hotspur	42	17	10	15	64	65	61
West Ham United	42	17	9	16	60	55	60
Aston Villa	42	17	9	16	59	61	60
Watford	42	16	9	17	68	77	57
Ipswich Town	42	15	8	19	55	57	53
Sunderland	42	13	13	16	42	53	52
Norwich City	42	12	15	15	48	49	51
Leicester City	42	13	12	17	65	68	51
Luton Town	42	14	9	19	53	66	51
West Brom. Albion	42	14	9	19	48	62	51
Stoke City	42	13	11	18	44	63	50
Coventry City	42	13	11	18	57	77	50
Birmingham City	42	12	12	18	39	50	48
Notts County	42	10	11	21	50	72	41
Wolves	42	6	11	25	27	80	29

1984-85 SEASON

FIRST DIVISION

Everton	42	28	6	8	88	43	90
Liverpool	42	22	11	9	78	35	77
Tottenham Hotspur	42	23	8	11	78	51	77
Manchester United	42	22	10	10	77	47	76
Southampton	42	19	11	12	56	47	68
Chelsea	42	18	12	12	63	48	66
Arsenal	42	19	9	14	61	49	66
Sheffield Wednesday	42	17	14	11	58	45	65
Nottingham Forest	**42**	**19**	**7**	**16**	**56**	**48**	**64**
Aston Villa	42	15	11	16	60	60	56
Watford	42	14	13	15	81	71	55
West Brom	42	16	7	19	58	62	55
Luton Town	42	15	9	18	57	61	54
Newcastle United	42	13	13	16	55	70	52
Leicester City	42	15	6	21	65	73	51
West Ham United	42	13	12	17	51	68	51
Ipswich Town	42	13	11	18	46	57	50
Coventry City	42	15	5	22	47	64	50
QPR	42	13	11	18	53	72	50
Norwich City	42	13	10	19	46	64	49
Sunderland	42	10	10	22	40	62	40
Stoke City	42	3	8	31	24	91	17

70

1985-86 SEASON
FIRST DIVISION

Liverpool	42	26	10	6	89	37	88
Everton	42	26	8	8	87	41	86
West Ham United	42	26	6	10	74	40	84
Manchester United	42	22	10	10	70	36	76
Sheffield Wednesday	42	21	10	11	63	54	73
Chelsea	42	20	11	11	57	56	71
Arsenal	42	20	9	13	49	47	69
Nottingham Forest	**42**	**19**	**11**	**12**	**69**	**53**	**68**
Luton Town	42	18	12	12	61	44	66
Tottenham Hotspur	42	19	8	15	74	52	65
Newcastle United	42	17	12	13	67	72	63
Watford	42	16	11	15	69	62	59
QPR	42	15	7	20	53	64	52
Southampton	42	12	10	20	51	62	46
Manchester City	42	11	12	19	43	57	45
Aston Villa	42	10	14	18	51	67	44
Coventry City	42	11	10	21	48	71	43
Oxford United	42	10	12	20	62	80	42
Leicester City	42	10	12	20	54	76	42
Ipswich Town	42	11	8	23	32	55	41
Birmingham City	42	8	5	29	30	73	29
West Brom	42	4	12	26	35	89	24

1986-87 SEASON
FIRST DIVISION

Everton	42	26	8	8	76	31	86
Liverpool	42	23	8	11	72	42	77
Tottenham Hotspur	42	21	8	13	68	43	71
Arsenal	42	20	10	12	58	35	70
Norwich City	42	17	17	8	53	51	68
Wimbledon	42	19	9	14	57	50	66
Luton Town	42	18	12	12	47	45	66
Nottingham Forest	**42**	**18**	**11**	**13**	**64**	**51**	**65**
Watford	42	18	9	15	67	54	63
Coventry City	42	17	12	13	50	45	63
Manchester United	42	14	14	14	52	45	56
Southampton	42	14	10	18	69	68	52
Sheffield Wednesday	42	13	13	16	58	59	52
Chelsea	42	13	13	16	53	64	52
West Ham United	42	14	10	18	52	67	52
QPR	42	13	11	18	48	64	50
Newcastle United	42	12	11	19	47	65	47
Oxford United	42	11	13	18	44	69	46
Charlton Athletic	42	11	11	20	45	55	44
Leicester City	42	11	9	22	54	76	42
Manchester City	42	8	15	19	36	57	39
Aston Villa	42	8	12	22	45	79	36

1987-88 SEASON
FIRST DIVISION

Liverpool	40	26	12	2	87	24	90
Manchester United	40	23	12	5	71	38	81
Nottingham Forest	**40**	**20**	**13**	**7**	**67**	**39**	**73**
Everton	40	19	13	8	53	27	70
QPR	40	19	10	11	48	38	67
Arsenal	40	18	12	10	58	39	66
Wimbledon	40	14	15	11	58	47	57
Newcastle United	40	14	14	12	55	53	56
Luton Town	40	14	11	15	57	58	53
Coventry City	40	13	14	13	46	53	53
Sheffield Wednesday	40	15	8	17	52	66	53
Southampton	40	12	14	14	49	53	50
Tottenham Hotspur	40	12	11	17	38	48	47
Norwich City	40	12	9	19	40	52	45
Derby County	40	10	13	17	35	45	43
West Ham United	40	9	15	16	40	52	42
Charlton Athletic	40	9	15	16	38	52	42
Chelsea	40	9	15	16	50	68	42
Portsmouth	40	7	14	19	36	66	35
Watford	40	7	11	22	27	51	32
Oxford United	40	6	13	21	44	80	31

1988-89 SEASON
FIRST DIVISION

Arsenal	38	22	10	6	73	36	76
Liverpool	38	22	10	6	65	28	76
Nottingham Forest	**38**	**17**	**13**	**8**	**64**	**43**	**64**
Norwich City	38	17	11	10	48	45	62
Derby County	38	17	7	14	40	38	58
Tottenham Hotspur	38	15	12	11	60	46	57
Coventry City	38	14	13	11	47	42	55
Everton	38	14	12	12	50	45	54
QPR	38	14	11	13	43	37	53
Millwall	38	14	11	13	47	52	53
Manchester United	38	13	12	13	45	35	51
Wimbledon	38	14	9	15	50	46	51
Southampton	38	10	15	13	52	66	45
Charlton Athletic	38	10	12	16	44	58	42
Sheffield Wednesday	38	10	12	16	34	51	42
Luton Town	38	10	11	17	42	52	41
Aston Villa	38	9	13	16	45	56	40
Middlesbrough	38	9	12	17	44	61	39
West Ham United	38	10	8	20	37	62	38
Newcastle United	38	7	10	21	32	63	31

1989-90 SEASON
FIRST DIVISION

Liverpool	38	23	10	5	78	37	79
Aston Villa	38	21	7	10	57	38	70
Tottenham Hotspur	38	19	6	13	59	47	63
Arsenal	38	18	8	12	54	38	62
Chelsea	38	16	12	10	58	50	60
Everton	38	17	8	13	51	33	59
Southampton	38	15	10	13	71	63	55
Wimbledon	38	13	16	9	47	40	55
Nottingham Forest	**38**	**15**	**9**	**14**	**55**	**47**	**54**
Norwich City	38	13	14	11	44	42	53
QPR	38	13	11	14	45	44	50
Coventry City	38	14	7	17	39	59	49
Manchester United	38	13	9	16	46	47	48
Manchester City	38	12	12	14	43	52	48
Crystal Palace	38	13	9	16	42	66	48
Derby County	38	13	7	18	43	40	46
Luton Town	38	10	13	15	43	57	43
Sheffield Wednesday	38	11	10	17	35	51	43
Charlton Athletic	38	7	9	22	31	57	30
Millwall	38	5	11	22	39	65	26

1990-91 SEASON

FIRST DIVISION

Arsenal	38	24	13	1	74	18	83
Liverpool	38	23	7	8	77	40	76
Crystal Palace	38	20	9	9	50	41	69
Leeds United	38	19	7	12	65	47	64
Manchester City	38	17	11	10	64	53	62
Manchester United	38	16	12	10	58	45	59
Wimbledon	38	14	14	10	53	46	56
Nottingham Forest	**38**	**14**	**12**	**12**	**65**	**50**	**54**
Everton	38	13	12	13	50	46	51
Tottenham	38	11	16	11	51	50	49
Chelsea	38	13	10	15	58	69	49
QPR	38	12	10	16	44	53	46
Sheffield United	38	13	7	18	36	55	46
Southampton	38	12	9	17	58	69	45
Norwich City	38	13	6	19	41	64	45
Coventry City	38	11	11	16	42	49	44
Aston Villa	38	9	14	15	46	58	41
Luton Town	38	10	7	21	42	61	37
Sunderland	38	8	10	20	38	60	34
Derby County	38	5	9	24	37	75	24

Arsenal 2 points deducted
Manchester United 1 point deducted

1991-92 SEASON

FIRST DIVISION

Leeds United	42	22	16	4	74	37	82
Manchester United	42	21	15	6	63	33	78
Sheffield Wednesday	42	21	12	9	62	49	75
Arsenal	42	19	15	8	81	46	72
Manchester City	42	20	10	12	61	48	70
Liverpool	42	16	16	10	47	40	64
Aston Villa	42	17	9	16	48	44	60
Nottingham Forest	**42**	**16**	**11**	**15**	**60**	**58**	**59**
Sheffield United	42	16	9	17	65	63	57
Crystal Palace	42	14	15	13	53	61	57
QPR	42	12	18	12	48	47	54
Everton	42	13	14	15	52	51	53
Wimbledon	42	13	14	15	53	53	53
Chelsea	42	13	14	15	50	60	53
Tottenham	42	15	7	20	58	63	52
Southampton	42	14	10	18	39	55	52
Oldham Athletic	42	14	9	19	63	67	51
Norwich City	42	11	12	19	47	63	45
Coventry City	42	11	11	20	35	44	44
Luton Town	42	10	12	20	38	71	42
Notts County	42	10	10	22	40	62	40
West Ham United	42	9	11	22	37	59	38

1992-93 SEASON

PREMIER DIVISION

Manchester United	42	24	12	6	67	31	84
Aston Villa	42	21	11	10	57	40	74
Norwich City	42	21	9	12	61	65	72
Blackburn Rovers	42	20	11	11	68	46	71
QPR	42	17	12	13	63	55	63
Liverpool	42	16	11	15	62	55	59
Sheffield Wednesday	42	15	14	13	55	51	59
Tottenham	42	16	11	15	60	66	59
Manchester City	42	15	12	15	56	51	57
Arsenal	42	15	11	16	40	38	56
Chelsea	42	14	14	14	51	54	56
Wimbledon	42	14	12	16	56	55	54
Everton	42	15	8	19	53	55	53
Sheffield United	42	14	10	18	54	53	52
Coventry City	42	13	13	16	52	57	52
Ipswich Town	42	12	16	14	50	55	52
Leeds United	42	12	15	15	57	62	51
Southampton	42	13	11	18	54	61	50
Oldham Athletic	42	13	10	19	63	74	49
Crystal Palace	42	11	16	15	48	61	49
Middlesbrough	42	11	11	20	54	75	44
Nottingham Forest	**42**	**10**	**10**	**22**	**41**	**62**	**40**

1993-94 SEASON

FIRST DIVISION

Crystal Palace	46	27	9	10	73	46	90
Nottingham Forest	**46**	**23**	**14**	**9**	**74**	**49**	**83**
Millwall	46	19	17	10	58	49	74
Leicester City	46	19	16	11	72	59	73
Tranmere Rovers	46	21	9	16	69	53	72
Derby County	46	20	11	15	73	68	71
Notts County	46	20	7	9	65	69	68
Wolves	46	17	17	12	60	47	68
Middlesbrough	46	18	13	15	66	54	67
Stoke City	46	18	13	15	57	59	67
Charlton Athletic	46	19	8	19	61	58	65
Sunderland	46	19	8	19	54	57	65
Bristol City	46	16	16	14	47	50	64
Bolton Wanderers	46	15	14	17	63	64	59
Southend United	46	17	8	21	63	67	59
Grimsby Town	46	13	20	13	52	47	59
Portsmouth	46	15	13	18	52	58	58
Barnsley	46	16	7	23	55	67	55
Watford	46	15	9	22	66	80	54
Luton Town	46	14	11	21	56	60	53
West Brom. Albion	46	13	12	21	60	69	51
Birmingham City	46	13	12	21	52	69	51
Oxford United	46	13	10	23	54	75	49
Peterborough United	46	8	13	25	48	76	37

1994-95 SEASON

F.A. PREMIERSHIP

Blackburn Rovers	42	27	8	7	80	39	89
Manchester United	42	26	10	6	77	28	88
Nottingham Forest	**42**	**22**	**11**	**9**	**72**	**43**	**77**
Liverpool	42	21	11	10	65	37	74
Leeds United	42	20	13	9	59	38	63
Newcastle United	42	20	12	10	67	47	72
Tottenham Hotspur	42	16	14	12	66	58	62
QPR	42	17	9	16	61	59	60
Wimbledon	42	15	11	16	48	65	56
Southampton	42	12	18	12	61	63	54
Chelsea	42	13	15	14	50	55	54
Arsenal	42	13	12	17	52	49	51
Sheffield Wednesday	42	13	12	17	49	57	51
West Ham United	42	13	11	18	44	48	50
Everton	42	11	17	14	44	51	50
Coventry City	42	12	14	16	44	62	50
Manchester City	42	12	13	17	53	64	49
Aston Villa	42	11	15	16	51	56	48
Crystal Palace	42	11	12	19	34	49	45
Norwich City	42	10	13	19	37	54	43
Leicester City	42	6	11	25	45	80	29
Ipswich Town	42	7	6	29	36	93	27